KS3-4
LESSON PLANS

DRAMA SCHEMES
BY MARK WHEELLER

RHINEGOLD
EDUCATION

www.rhinegoldeducation.co.uk

Drama Study Guides
AS and A2 Drama Study Guide (Edexcel), AS and A2 Drama Study Guide (AQA),
GCSE Drama Study Guide (Edexcel)
Also available from Rhinegold Education
Baroque Music in Focus, Film Music in Focus, Musicals in Focus

First published 2010 in Great Britain by
Rhinegold Education
14–15 Berners Street
London W1T 3LJ, UK
www.rhinegoldeducation.co.uk

© Rhinegold Publishing Ltd 2010
a division of Music Sales Limited.

Drama Schemes by Mark Wheeller
Order No. RHG523
ISBN: 978-1-907447-17-4

Exclusive Distributors:
Music Sales Limited, Distribution Centre, Newmarket Road,
Bury St Edmunds, Suffolk IP33 3YB, UK.

Printed in the EU.

Contents

Acknowledgements

My family, Jean and John Wheeller (mum and dad), Rachael (wife) and children Ollie, Charlie and Daisy who have all had to put up with my addiction to work (or exam-work avoidance in my childhood) at some stage.

David Cooke, Dave Goldring and Barbie Stone (Davies): Marlwood School. *Tony Key:* 4R Movement and Dance Group and Goldsmiths' College.

Various drama teachers I have worked with who have influenced my work, *Luke Abbott, James Fishwick and Roy Nevitt from Stantonbury Campus, Roger Parsley, Essex drama advisor to St John's in Epping, Clare Clegg; St John's, Jonny Carrington; Oaklands/ Oasis, Ken Taylor & Andy Kempe.*

All my head teachers who have given me the opportunity to be imaginative (so many drama teachers don't seem to have this freedom) *Geoff Cooksey (Stantonbury Campus,) Stan Dixon (St John's in Epping), Pete Hollis/Sarah Howells (Oaklands Community School) and Ian Golding (Oasis Academy Lord's Hill)*

Various (guru) practitioners who in my early years of teaching inspired me to new heights: *Dorothy Heathcote, Gavin Bolton, Cecily O'Neill, Jonothan Neelands, Peter Cheeseman, & Brian Way.*

Ex students and youth theatre members over the years: there are far too many to name but these people have taught me so much. It has been so rewarding to meet up with them again in the internet age! They've suffered my experiments and mad ideas with amazing courage!

Ginny Spooner: chief examiner, Edexcel GCSE.

Ape and StopWatch theatre companies for their ongoing work performing my plays in schools. In particular *Matt & Yvonne Allen, Adrian New & Steve Pearce.*

Meg Davies and Sophie Gorell Barnes: MBA Literary Agents.

Dawn Boyfield, Evie Efthimiou & Lynda Taylor: dbda for taking on my plays when most other publishers wouldn't!

Graham Salmon and the various other people who have inspired the content of my plays.

Foreword

Let's not feel too sorry that Mark Wheeller's early ambitions of becoming an astronaut, footballer or pop star never came to fruition. Perhaps he would have been a great success at any one of those but we'll never know and anyway, it doesn't really matter because he's managed to follow the best career advice there is: find something you enjoy doing, and do it to the best of your ability. This book is a fine representation of what Mark not only enjoys doing but does very well. As a drama teacher, he has an ability to explain things clearly and employ a wide range of imaginative strategies to explore issues and help students create vibrant pieces of theatre. As a playwright he has developed a set of effective formulae for dramatising real events while leaving space for young performers to experiment and express themselves in new and engaging ways. Underlying both of these professional personas is, quite simply, a great sense of drama and the dramatic. It is a sense that allows him to make drama lesson feel like plays, while his plays serve as a vehicle for teaching lessons in both content and form.

Mark's preface mentions how limited the opportunities were for him in terms of a drama education when he was at school. The old style drama 'lesson' in which the teacher abdicated all responsibility to teach anything about anything and just left students to embarrass themselves and each other with their own ill-informed devices, will doubtless be all too horribly familiar to many. Fortunately, because of teachers like Mark, things have moved on and those who want to actually teach young people how to get better at drama now have resources like this book on which to draw. Mark generously acknowledges the debt he owes to Roy Nevitt and Luke Abbott and it is good to see the legacy of these two brilliant teachers reaching a wider audience through the way Mark has synthesised their work in theatre and pedagogy. Perhaps he has been blessed with the ability to be in the right place at the right time with the right people, though in some ways this might have felt like a mixed blessing. Certainly, it must have been a privilege to have known athlete Graham Salmon, the eponymous hero of *Graham: World's Fastest Blind Runner*, though a harrowing experience getting to know the family whose story is told in *Dan Nolan: Missing*. However, in both of these cases, as with other plays he has written, Mark has an extraordinary capacity to spot dramatic potential then utilise his understanding of theatre and his knowledge of drama pedagogy to give it life and import on the stage and in the classroom. Citing another major influence on his work, Mark notes how he was able to imagine what one of Dorothy Heathcote's lessons looked liked from the way it was described. A great strength of this book rests in how Mark describes his teaching methods and his practical ideas so clearly that drama teachers new and old will be able to adopt and adapt them with ease.

A good drama lesson needs to be about something that feels interesting and worth exploring. It also needs to extend the students' appreciation of, and skills in, the art form we call drama. A fundamental question drama teachers therefore persistently need to ask themselves when they are planning and delivering drama lessons is, 'where's the drama?' For a plethora of examples of how to answer this question, read on ...

Andy Kempe

UNIVERSITY OF READING, JULY 2010

I didn't always want to be a drama teacher, and never really had any ambition to be a playwright. So what were my ambitions? When I was six or seven years old, I wrote in a school magazine: 'I want to be an astronaut' (every 1960's child's dream). That dream was short-lived; throughout my secondary school years I wanted to be a footballer and then a pop star. I rose to the dizzy heights of playing (occasionally) for my school football team but worked much harder on the pop star ambition, sadly with little success. I wrote music to literally hundreds of songs with various friends penning the lyrics as I didn't feel I was good with words. I had a decent voice and (over)confidence on stage so I had these assets to bargain with.

I struck a deal with a local band seeking a singer; I would honour them with my voice and grand stage presence on the condition that they performed two of my songs in their set. The arrangement lasted for just two gigs. I don't recall anyone walking out or jeering but I decided to leave due to 'musical differences' and find my fame and fortune writing the music for original musicals just like Lionel Bart and Andrew Lloyd Webber had done. It was this path that would eventually lead me to write my own plays.

My relations had made it very clear that my superstar ambitions were not realistic so when asked: 'what are you going to be when you grow up?' I proffered another, more acceptable answer: 'I want to be a teacher'. Although teaching was perhaps a 'back-up' plan to my fantasy, it was something I had held a genuine interest in for a long time.

My dad was a music teacher and his dad before him an English teacher, so perhaps it's in the genes. I remember having a blackboard and easel for my sixth birthday. I woke up my poor parents most mornings for the next year or so, enthusiastically teaching them what I had learnt the previous day, before heading off to school. They tell me I was a hard taskmaster but enjoyed the process of sharing what I had learnt. They were very tolerant of my eccentricities even in those early days!

I was a 'naughty' (cheeky rather than wicked) schoolboy and remember thinking how badly some of my teachers dealt with my own misbehaviour. However, I was equally aware when a teacher gained my respect and found it normally came down to the basics of relationships. Does this mean they couldn't be strict? No, far from it; there's not much worse than a teacher who has no control. My maths teacher was very much of the 'old school'; she was a strict disciplinarian, but I knew she cared and that my progress mattered to her. Miss Walker dragged me through my CSE Maths and I am forever in her debt for doing so – she was an outstanding teacher. At that age, I remember analysing teachers and thinking how easy it seemed; it came down to being caring, consistent, honest, approachable and – last but not least – having high expectations.

As a 14 year old, my career seemed a long way off and I had absolutely no idea what subject I would/could teach. I knew so little of anything other than being able to recite the hits of David Bowie and their various chart positions (I still can!), and a good working knowledge of football league tables/teams. However, I wasn't that interested in the formal side of music and being a sports teacher seemed much too tiring and would also require interest in sport well beyond football! In the sixth form I had to decide what subject I would teach to complete my teacher training college application form. I remember looking down the list and thinking: 'I can't, and wouldn't want to do any of these subjects!' The only one I felt might be vaguely possible was one I had no experience in: drama.

My school had offered me limited opportunities in drama to say the least. In the third year (Year 9) we were allowed to take drama, as a treat, once in a blue moon. These lessons involved us emptying out dressing up boxes and wearing (mostly women's) clothing, putting on odd, high-pitched Monty Python voices and presenting short comedic (or not!) performances while the teacher sat and did her marking. I had wanted to get involved in school productions but was thrown out because my behaviour in English was so poor. So for me, at this point, drama equalled a treat that could be taken away from you at the drop of a hat and, from my observations of the teacher, it seemed that anyone could do this ... yes, even me! I duly ticked the drama box and felt this could be an easy career decision.

It was in that final term of my lower sixth form that I directed my first original musical production as part of a celebration I organised to bid farewell to a favourite teacher of mine. *Hardened Criminals* was actually little more than an opportunity to get five of my songs performed within the context of a play that I managed to talk my then girlfriend into writing. Having given up on the pop star ambition I decided I could become the next Andrew Lloyd Webber. No one was prepared to organise the actors so, spurred on by the fact I was preparing to become a drama teacher, I also took on the role of director and I loved it.

The success of this initial production led me to direct two more in my final year at school as part of my new-found role as house captain. There was so much interest generated in these productions that people from other houses wanted to be involved. It was incredible, and gave me the opportunity to write more songs which would be performed. The downside from my parent's point of view was that they distracted me from my studies. Fortunately I was able to get on a Certificate in Education course in drama with an unconditional offer (without having to pass any A levels). The experience of putting on these productions was, in my view, much more valuable than some irrelevant A levels!

Another really useful influence was the local Thornbury Amateur Operatic Society (TAOS) where my dad was the musical director. Starting off as Call Boy in *Hello Dolly,* I progressed to 2nd Policeman in the pantomime *Aladdin* ... a named part in the programme! I felt like a celebrity; people who had seen the TAOS productions recognised me in the local International Stores supermarket where I worked on Saturdays. Obviously this was exactly the sort of grounding any budding drama teacher needed. Perhaps this was going to be as exciting as being a pop star!

At the start of my final school year my status as the drama guru of our school was challenged. They appointed Barbie Stone (later Davies) as a specialist drama teacher. Barbie was, I think, bemused (or perhaps amused) by what I was up to – directing these home grown musicals, but didn't interfere with what I was doing. Everyone loved her and she won me over completely. She was different to all the other teachers – younger and far more approachable. She put drama on the map at our school (Marlwood Comprehensive in Alveston, Bristol) and proved to be the final piece in the jigsaw in making me see that this was not necessarily an easy career, but certainly an interesting one to aspire to. Once my A levels were over (and failed!) I spent all my free time working with Barbie, teaching drama to the younger students; I loved it, and knew this job was going to be fun, fun, fun!

In my three years training to be a teacher I found the educational drama preparation appalling. I was on the middle years Cert. Ed. course and so only had a short, one hour a week, six-week course to train me in my specialism – unbelievable! The remainder was training to be a middle years teacher, with one day a week doing drama 'at our own level' ... which was unfortunately well beyond mine. I was, however, introduced to the work of Harold Pinter and remember being very taken by his efforts to make speech in his plays real; I became sufficiently interested to focus on his work for my special study; other than this, though, it all passed me by.

What *did* capture my interest at this time was the 4R Movement and Dance Group based in Lewisham and run by a movement lecturer at my college, Tony Key. He was even filmed for the BBC's Horizon programme (although it was never broadcast). 4R had casts of well over 100 who performed at the 1000-seat Lewisham Concert Hall (where David Bowie once presented Ziggy Stardust!). I had no interest in dance but Tony made it accessible and a wide range of youngsters were involved alongside their parents – a fabulous example of what I would come to know as Community Theatre. He taught me to how to get the best out of a large cast and valued our opinions, often using cast members' ideas to stage scenes. I still use this method when directing shows, gaining a huge sense of commitment/loyalty from the cast, just as Tony did. Tony brought me in as a songwriter and for the first time the group used live music, played by the college's music department orchestra, organised by a friend of mine. Working with Tony and 4R proved to be the most inspiring experience of my college years.

Tony made the 4R productions seem important, probably far more than they actually were. The scale of them contributed to this. He borrowed or hired sets from Pinewood Studios (which involved us visiting the studio) and on one memorable occasion brought in 'Blakey' (Stephen Lewis) from the (then) super popular TV series *On the Buses* to guest on the last night. Blakey had to sing one of my tunes ... it was unbelievable! The prestigious venues we performed at topped it all off. This sense of importance inspired an unusual level of commitment amongst all of us working with 4R. Looking back, I realise that this is something that I manage to generate within the groups I work with and it has become central feature in creating the success my youth theatres have had.

When it came to the end of my three years did not take up the option to do an extra year to convert my humble Cert. Ed. into a fully-fledged honours degree. Everyone said I would live to regret it ... I haven't. I was keen to get out and work 'in the field' and when I did, I landed on my feet. I was appointed as a drama teacher at the progressive Stantonbury Campus Secondary School in Milton Keynes. I had fully expected to be working in a department of one (myself) making up what I did as I went along, learning from various books and occasional courses. Instead I had four other experienced drama teachers working alongside me. They introduced me to someone my college had never even mentioned: Dorothy Heathcote. At Stantonbury I heard nothing *but* Dorothy Heathcote and lapped it up. I was introduced to her methodology by Luke Abbott, now internationally renowned for his Mantle of the Expert work utilising and further developing Dorothy's teaching strategy. Luke was my curriculum head of department. He introduced me to use teacher-in-role and that became my modus operandi for all my drama lessons.

To support this teaching I read *Drama as a Learning Medium* by Betty Jane Wagner. This is a fantastic account of Dorothy's working practice written in accessible language. I remember reading the account of Heathcote working in-role as a ghost who didn't know how to play. She was working with some very young children who ended up teaching the ghost to play and, in doing so, deconstructed the skills they already had. This was so well-written that I was able to imagine it clearly even though I had not actually witnessed it.

At Stantonbury I learned how to teach. I was given the opportunity to team-teach with one of the drama teachers for two hours a week, providing me with an amazing on-the-job training (and something I've tried to do with any incoming drama teacher at my school). The teachers were all called by first names (including the head teacher). I have held onto this throughout my career as I believe it makes for a much more positive and respectful relationship between student and teacher. I am amazed this does not happen in other schools as it seems so much more natural to me.

'We try to avoid artificial barriers between students and the adults they work with. Everyone on Campus is known by their first name. Students are used to having their opinions listened to and valued. This creates a rich inclusive environment for learning and friendly relationships between adults and students.'

Stantonbury Campus Prospectus 2010.

Stantonbury was also one of the first schools to have carpeted classrooms which are now de rigueur in all schools. First names next then?

At Stantonbury I was introduced to another idea which became a huge influence in my work. The director of drama, Roy Nevitt, was renowned for his Documentary Theatre work. Roy's philosophy was to put bums on seats by telling stories from the local community. 'Dig where you stand' was his motto.

Milton Keynes in the late seventies/early eighties was a particularly interesting city to test out this ideology. Uniquely, it had no shared history amongst its communities. Few of those who lived there had done so for much longer than a few months or years. Roy developed productions which, in my view, helped this infant city to gain a sense of identity. They were incredibly successful at drawing interest from the local community and beyond, often capturing the imagination of local television. In the same way that Roy used stories from history, I later went on to dramatise contemporary stories, but never while I was at Stantonbury. During my time there I served up a diet of homemade large-cast musicals, never daring to copy my mentor on his own patch!

I stayed at Stantonbury for three years and was then promoted to head of department at St John's Comprehensive School in Epping, which had no history of drama and very few facilities for the subject. I remember on my interview day the outgoing drama teacher said to me: 'You will never get drama going at this place.' The contrast with Stantonbury could not have been more pronounced and I could not have been more determined to succeed. While I was there I was able to apply many of the ideas I had learnt from Stantonbury and developed a number of successful schemes of work, two of which appear in this book. *Too Much Punch for Judy*, my first really successful docu-play, was created in my final year there. My time in Epping consolidated my experiences and allowed me to apply them in a different setting. It also, once again, provided me with many very good memories and, five years later, I left a well-established and highly-respected department behind me.

After Epping I moved to Southampton where I took on a very exciting role in Oaklands Community School, which already had a successful drama department and a wonderful theatre. It seemed in so many ways to be a mini Stantonbury and a job I didn't expect to get at the tender age of 29! My intention was to stay there for five years and move on but I have enjoyed my time here so much that I have stayed and now find myself one of the oldest and longest-serving staff members.

Longevity has many benefits. One of my greatest thrills at this school has been welcoming back members from the Oaklands' Youth Theatre group (OYT). Danny Sturrock is but one example of this; five years after he left, Danny came back and greeted me with a play he'd written, which he wanted OYT to present. *Gagging For It* (much admired GCSE/A level text., DBDA, 1995) remains one of my favourite plays ever and I am very proud to have had some part in its genesis. Since then, Danny has been a valuable member of OYT, having contributed multimedia to my own productions and is developing a number of his own. His input has developed and modernised OYT more than I could ever have done on my own. Had I moved on Danny may never have returned as he wouldn't have known who to go to, and I would be working with an ever-changing group of young people with little consistency. Danny is one of many who have returned to OYT and we are much the richer for it. For Danny's part, he gave up a successful career in the finance industry to pursue his dream of becoming a film maker; he is currently working towards a degree in media studies.

Oaklands Community School has recently endured the uncertainties of transition, merging with another school and by becoming an academy, which has – in the end – worked out particularly well for me. I continue to play an important role in developing the newly-named Oasis Academy Lord's Hill, running the Oasis Youth Theatre (fortunately the acronym is still OYT), teaching drama and increasingly attempting to take drama methodology into other areas of the curriculum. The academy has a philosophy that welcomes creativity. Our drama department staff and students are all encouraged to develop new and interesting work. We constantly seek to push the boundaries.

My decision to tick that drama box on the teacher-training form with no relevant experience has led me to a fulfilling career. Not having an academic grounding in traditional theatre, I have had to create my own style of work from experiences I have had. This has led me to an interesting area of expertise ... that of the work of Mark Wheeller. I feel I am well-placed to espouse that expertise!

What follows is an account of some of my favourite lessons, one for each secondary school year, a kind of 'greatest hits'. These schemes are based on those used when preparing for, or working on, the Edexcel GCSE exam, which is what I have taught for the last 22 years. They have all been generalised so that they not specific to any GCSE exam board, and should be of use to all. I hope there are some 'hit' lessons yet to come; in fact, I am convinced that is the case. I am beginning to explore ways to develop Mantle of the Expert and have included an early attempt at this work as one of the schemes in this book, so I like to think of this as more of a drama schemes greatest hits ... the early years!

Mark Wheeller

Wacky Soap

Although this scheme of work is suggested for Year 7 it works well with other age groups, both younger and older.

Introduction

There have been countless features on the TV asking how substance-abuse education can be broached with the very young. The following scheme is based on a fictional, mind-altering substance, 'wacky soap', which produces euphoric, wacky sensations in the user along with some very troubling physical side-effects. It approaches the difficult subject of substance abuse in an oblique way, thereby removing much of the controversy associated with it. It is what Luke Abbott at Stantonbury used to call 'protecting into the material'. This scheme could be used as much as a health education project as a drama one and will work effectively both in a classroom and a drama space.

The scheme uses my musical *Wacky Soap* as its basis. It's an enjoyable, fun story and I believe that if you enjoy something you will want to talk about the issues surrounding it. Discussion with careful teacher intervention is one way to create an environment where effective learning can occur. It is an allegorical story; allegory enables people of all ages to think freshly about any subject. When discussing substance abuse, everybody arrives with their existing preconceptions and opinions set in concrete, well before any discussion begins. The questions this allegory prompts may, in some cases, cause students to re-evaluate their attitudes. They will be able to apply the answers they come up with to real-life situations. I am not saying that participating in this scheme will stop students from abusing substances – be it cigarettes, alcohol, illegal drugs, butane gas or anything else – but it does raise important issues and, by looking at these from a new perspective and through a fictional product, it will encourage more honest debates.

Background to *Wacky Soap*

James Thurber, 'The Bear Who Let It Alone', *Fables for our Time* (1983, Harper Perennial).

Wacky Soap started out life as a small part of my play *Quenchers,* a series of short scenes showing the different facets of alcohol misuse. The finale to *Quenchers* was a dramatic section on drink-driving, telling the story of Judy Poulton; this scene was so powerful that I later developed it into a one-act play, *Too Much Punch for Judy*. Because of its upsetting content, I wanted it to be preceded by a light-hearted, funny piece. I had come across a short story called 'The Bear Who Let It Alone' by James Thurber and wanted to adapt this. Unfortunately (fortunately, in retrospect) James Thurber's estate would not grant permission for this so I was forced to quickly create a comic alternative of my own.

Using the allegorical nature of Thurber's story I decided to incorporate *Monty Python*-style characters into my invention, their incongruity contributing additional humour to the story. Thus, the characters of the smelly biker-queen and the princess who dies and does not come back to life were born. The original story in *Quenchers* was not as developed as this final incarnation, but I recognised that it had potential and included it as an appendix in the first edition of *Too Much Punch for Judy*. I subsequently turned what was then a four-page story into a 20-page one-act play which, in 1992, was presented by the Oaklands Youth Theatre in Southampton. A few years later I was working with the composer James Holmes on *The Most Absurd Promenade Xmas Musical in the World … Ever!*. I recognised that his style of songwriting (which I would describe as 'Disneyesque') suited the story of *Wacky Soap* perfectly. Soon we were developing it into a musical, and so *Wacky Soap: A Cautionary Tale* was born. It has now become my most performed musical, as it is perfectly suited to drama club-type productions.

Wacky Soap in the classroom

Reworking *Wacky Soap* revived my interest in a scheme of work I had developed back in Epping in the days of *Quenchers*. This was one of those rare schemes which dealt with a serious subject in a comic manner. I have used the *Wacky Soap* scheme as part of our Year 7 curriculum for many years but I have also used it (or variants of it) with students from the ages of 7 to 18. It always goes down well and students who have left often say they remember it as being one of their personal favourites.

Our production was short-listed for the National Theatre Lloyds Theatre Challenge and I won the Adjudicator's Award at the Totton One Act Drama Festival (part of the All England Theatre Festival) for writing the play.

Wacky Soap: A Cautionary Tale, Mark Wheeller & James Holmes (dbda, 1999).

It is also complemented by a wonderful, colour-illustrated story book. This contains some great ideas for costumes. *The Story of Wacky Soap: A Cautionary Tale*, Mark Wheeller, Rachel Wheeller, illus. Geoff Greiggs (dbda, 2001).

Wacky Soap

The scheme

This scheme, in various ways, addresses the following questions:

>> Imagine that Wacky Soap really had been invented. Would you want to try it?

>> If you had children, would you want to protect them from it? Would you let them try it, or would you turn a blind eye if they did?

>> How would you teach your children about its potential dangers? Would you talk to them about it? Or, perhaps you would never talk to them about Wacky Soap, leaving them ignorant about it?

>> How would you feel if your children temporarily lost a limb (or two)?

>> Worse still, how would you cope if someone you loved washed themselves away completely?

>> Should the government be allowed to make money from Wacky Soap? If so (as in the full-length version of the story), how should that money be spent? Should the government make it illegal?

I imagine some may look at *Wacky Soap* and consider it to be aimed at KS2. There have been a few teachers of KS2 who have dared to take it on, but some of the songs can prove difficult. If you take a *Monty Python* approach to the musical, it becomes very much a secondary school-age production. Sixth form colleges often present it as a BTEC production.

One aspect that we had great fun with when we presented it in my school was the set; we used a bouncy castle for King Huff to deliver his speeches from. One of my friends, Tim Ford, came to see the production we did in Southampton and gave me a wonderful idea which I hope that someone, someday, may be able to achieve. He suggested that *Wacky Soap* could be performed in a swimming pool with inflatable props – what a production that would be! If I were to stage it again I might dress the narrator up as Trusty the Rubber Duck (who appears in the storybook). Whatever you choose to do with the staging of *Wacky Soap*, have fun with it!

Outline of scheme structure

>> Introduction to the story, confirming students' understanding through short performances

>> Spontaneous improvisation (in pairs) exploring some issues the story raises

>> Small group play-making/freeze-frames, dealing with marketing and warnings about Wacky Soap

Resources

Colour-illustrated story book - *The Story of Wacky Soap: A Cautionary Tale*, Mark and Rachel Wheeller, illustrated by Geoffrey Greiggs (2001, *dbda*)

Script - *Wacky Soap: A Cautionary Tale*, Mark Wheeller (1999, *dbda*)

CD soundtrack - *Wacky Soap*, Mark Wheeller and music by James Holmes (1999, *dbda*) (this is optional)

*All of the above can be purchased from dbda – www.dbda. co.uk

A means of projecting the colour illustrations from the storybook (laptop or overhead projector)

A variety of colour posters for health education/safety campaigns; these can be obtained from **www. thinkroadsafety.gov. uk**, **www.rospa.com** or **www.dh.gov.uk** (search for 'posters')

Laptop (optional)

Camcorder (optional)

Role cards for the whole class role-play (optional).

>> Whole-class role-play exploring the location of a Wacky Soap factory

>> Suggested extension activities.

Learning objectives

>> To explore through allegory issues surrounding substance misuse

>> To experience a variety of different ways of working

>> To develop skills of spontaneous role-play

>> To develop skills associated with taking on predetermined roles in a structured role-play exercise

>> To evaluate their own and others' work by watching filmed recordings of their performances

>> To perform in front of a larger audience than their own class (optional).

Allegory is particularly useful as it strips students of the baggage they arrive with and allows them to explore old issues afresh. I would normally encourage students to figure out what the deeper meanings are for themselves.

Cross-curricular links

Some suggestions for linked work in other subject areas:

>> **Music**: composition of Wacky Soap jingles or warning songs

>> **Art/IT**: poster design of Wacky Soap logos, packaging, advertising and warning campaigns

>> **Science**: exploration of mind-altering substances in the real world

>> **Media studies:** an animated version of the story.

Lessons 1 and 2

Learning objectives

>> To reproduce the *Wacky Soap* story

>> To work effectively in groups and communicate the story using prepared improvisation.

Read the *Wacky Soap* story

Read the following text to the class. When I tell the class the *Wacky Soap* story I always show Geoff Greiggs' illustrations from the story book on a screen from a laptop or overhead projector.

Once there was a king called King Huff. He ruled over the Bower of Bliss with Queen Huff, who was smelly, and their daughter the Princess Symbol, who was beautiful. The people of the Bower of Bliss were sensible and happy. However, King Huff wanted more than this for his people. He worked for three years to invent some soap with special powers to make his people wacky and therefore happier.

King Huff spoke to the people of the Bower of Bliss:

> 'Speedily step into your shower
> And wonder at Wacky Soap's power
> When you lather your skin
> You will giggle and grin
> And it will stop you from smelling so sour!'.

Immediately everyone tore off their clothes to wash with Wacky Soap. The effect was amazing! Everyone became sweet-scented and started acting in a wacky way. They pretended to be elephants and marched up and down the streets trumpeting loudly. It was very funny. But, unknown to the king, Wacky Soap had another power …

Wacky Soap also washed bits of people away. Some people washed away their arms. Some washed away their legs. Some washed away their heads. Some even washed away their naughty bits.

Princess Symbol liked Wacky Soap so much that she washed herself away, never to return. Her parents, King and Queen Huff, were heartbroken.

> 'What has happened here I truly regret,' exclaimed King Huff, 'Wacky Soap is a deadly threat!'.

The people of the Bower of Bliss were angry with their king.

> 'You said Wacky Soap would make us happier – wackier', said a woman who had a gap between her tummy and her knees. 'Instead, it is making us disappear. Wacky Soap is making us very sad. Wacky Soap is bad, that's very clear!'

The people of the Bower of Bliss looked to King Huff for an answer – a sensible answer. King Huff stood and spoke into his royal microphone:

> 'I can't bring back those who are washed away but I can ban Wacky Soap and that ban starts today!'

The King carved a statue of Princess Symbol to remind everyone that true happiness can never be made. Underneath the statue King Huff inscribed the following words:

> 'Lasting happiness comes from within, not from a lather on your skin.'

King Huff and his queen looked out onto the statue in the Bower of Bliss market square and they smiled. Although still very sad, they believed that their people could now create their own happy ending.

SPEEDY RE-TELLING COMPETITION

Allocate all students into groups of five or six. Each group prepares to present the sequence of events in the *Wacky Soap* story in a speedy, under-two-minute version or through a few carefully-selected freeze-frames. I sometimes turn this into a competition: who can tell the story in the shortest amount of time while including all the salient moments in the narrative? I stress that I am looking for speed, not necessarily quality. What I intend to get by the end of this session is highly energetic, rehearsed work and evidence that all students have understood the story.

Lessons 3 and 4

Learning objectives

>> To explore issues relating to substance abuse

>> To work in, and maintain, a believable role.

Class discussion

Tell students that Wacky Soap has arrived in our country and been legalised. Through discussion, they should establish what the government's stance should be. What are the age restrictions? Do the government want to impose any other restrictions? The discussion can be in or out of role. The inclusion of a teacher-chaired discussion is crucial to the success of these activities.

Improvisations

The following improvisations can be conducted in either of the following ways:

>> Class work in small groups simultaneously with no one watching so that everyone has the experience at the same time

>> Volunteer groups perform spontaneously in front of the class; the performances are then used as common reference points for class discussion.

Alternatively, you could combine both of the above methods, by asking students to perform the improvisations in pairs, simultaneously, and then invite two students to model the scene (or selected scenes) in front of the class. I would suggest, however, that the two students should not be from the same working pair, to avoid the spontaneity evaporating from the scene.

IMPROVISATION 1 (PARENT AND SON/DAUGHTER):

While tidying their son/daughter's room a parent discovers a bar of Wacky Soap hidden away in a drawer. It is unopened and unused. Later that day the son/daughter arrives home from school. What does the parent say?

This improvisation can be repeated, with the parent having a different attitude towards Wacky Soap and the son/daughter having a different reason for hiding the soap in the drawer. You could write these attitudes/reasons on cards and give them to the improvisers prior to starting the scene.

The son/daughter's reasons could include:

>> They stole the bar of Wacky Soap and have not used it yet

>> They were given the bar of Wacky Soap and planned to use it tonight

>> They took the Wacky Soap away from a friend who they knew to be in danger of disappearing.

The parent's stance could be:

>> They never use Wacky Soap
>> They are a casual Wacky Soap user
>> Their best friend disappeared after misusing Wacky Soap.

IMPROVISATION 2 (PARENT AND SON/DAUGHTER):

Son/daughter returns home from a friend's party where Wacky Soap was used. His/her writing arm and hand is, as a consequence of Wacky Soap overuse, temporarily missing! On arrival home, although the offspring tries to conceal it, the parents finally notice their child's missing limb. How do they deal with this? Students could draw out the comic possibilities which are contained in the son/daughter's attempted concealment of their missing arm.

IMPROVISATION 3 (PARENT AND SON/DAUGHTER):

Will the parent send their son/daughter into school the following morning even though his/her arm and hand has not returned? This is discussed over breakfast. The scene could be repeated and the stakes raised, by introducing the fact that on the same morning the son/daughter is due to sit an external exam or much looked forward to school trip.

IMPROVISATION 4 (HEAD TEACHER AND STUDENT):

How would the head teacher react if the son/daughter arrives at school with a missing arm? This would be a clear indication of Wacky Soap use. What message would the head teacher's reaction give to other students in the school? Begin the improvisation from when the head teacher spots the student making their way to their classroom.

IMPROVISATION 5 (PARENT AND SON/DAUGHTER):

Would the parents allow their son/daughter to go, or take Wacky Soap, to such a party in the future? This will be influenced by the legalities which were established in the opening discussion.

It might also be interesting to try the scene with Wacky Soap being legal in the first instance, and illegal in the second.

IMPROVISATION 6 (PARENT AND SON/DAUGHTER):

Would the parents be prepared to buy 20–30 bars of Wacky Soap for their son/daughter's 16th birthday party, to be held in their own house? Play this scene twice with two different scenarios:
>> Wacky Soap is illegal
>> Wacky Soap is legal for over-16s.
Establish what the parent's attitude is to Wacky Soap: would they use it themselves? In either scenario the son/daughter asking his/her parent to purchase Wacky Soap, and for permission to use it, should present a highly challenging scene.

Evaluation

Evaluate the improvisations as a class, focusing on content, issues raised and how these might apply to our own world. Are there similar situations we face in the modern world today? Is Wacky Soap mirrored by anything real? Also ask students to comment positively on anyone's individual work in the role-plays.

Lesson 5

Learning objectives

>> To work in a group effectively

>> To communicate a story using prepared improvisation

>> To use skills/conventions (such as choral speaking) to highlight and convey a message in a presentation for TV

>> To evaluate their work after watching it on screen

>> To explore and evaluate the effectiveness of advertising and propaganda campaigns.

Resources: health and safety education posters

Small group play-making

Look at some examples of health and safety education/posters with the class, to see how they are made: what kind of images and language do they use? Students should get themselves into small groups (making sure that no one is left out) and devise one of the following:

>> A Wacky Soap advert for television to promote the product (the presentation should be limited to 90 seconds)

>> A health education campaign for television to warn people of the dangers of Wacky Soap (again, the presentation should be limited to 90 seconds).

Presentations should include:

>> A freeze-frame (tableau) at the beginning and end, and possibly one somewhere in the middle to highlight a moment of significance

>> Choral speaking and choral movement

>> A clearly stated slogan linked with Wacky Soap.

Students may also like to think about:

>> Song and dance or rhymes/raps

>> Slow motion.

For the less able/confident, both of these could be done as poster campaigns instead, created through tableau.

As both of these tasks are intended for television it provides an ideal opportunity to film the resultant presentations on camcorder and use them for evaluation purposes. Students love watching a recording of themselves perform and it proves to be a useful tool for improving work. Tableaux can also be digitally filmed and projected onto a screen for evaluation purposes.

If you want to focus on the health education implications of this lesson, you could ask students: how effective are such campaigns in dealing with these kind of issues? What other techniques are used to educate the public about substance abuse?

Lesson 6

Learning objectives

>> To explore issues relating to substance abuse

>> To maintain a role in a role-play.

Whole class role-play

Read students the following text:

> Wacky Soap Incorporated wish to build a new Wacky Soap factory in your community. It will be built on vacant land in the same road as the local junior school, secondary school and youth club. The Wacky Soap factory will bring in much-needed income to the town through rent, new employment and so on. A national protest group, Action Against Wacky Soap, who are campaigning to ban the product, are very angry about the proposal.
>
> Wacky Soap Inc.'s are aware of Wacky Soap's controversial nature and are prepared to provide some kind of facility for the community, for instance an ice rink. They may also be keen to sponsor classrooms in local schools. They will produce their own health education pack detailing the dangers of Wacky Soap and a guide to using it safely. These will be provided free of charge to schools.
>
> Many jobs will be provided for the local community. If the factory is not built here, there are contingency plans for it to be built elsewhere in the UK.

Tell the class that you are going to allocate roles and they are going to role-play a meeting at a local community centre, debating the proposed new Wacky Soap factory.

In a typical class of 30, roles could be allocated as follows:
>> One chair – possibly the teacher
>> Four members of the Wacky Soap Users Group, all of whom use Wacky Soap regularly
>> One managing director of Wacky Soap Inc.
>> One manager of the only other existing Wacky Soap factory in a similar community elsewhere. They have first-hand experience of establishing this type of venture successfully
>> One person appointed to become the new factory manager and who is responsible for appointing new staff from the local community
>> Two head teachers from the local junior and secondary schools
>> Two deputy head teachers – responsible for student welfare
>> One youth club leader
>> Four town councillors
>> Two local police
>> Five members of Action Against Wacky Soap.

You could produce more detailed role cards, should you wish.

Prior to the general meeting all students playing the same, or similar, roles should meet to decide on their response to the proposal (for instance, you could place the youth club leader with the two head teachers to discuss their position in respect to young people in the area).

Role-play the meeting to decide if the factory should be built in the community.

Extension activities

Teacher-in-role and playwright-on-the-edge

Experienced drama teachers may wish to explore the previous role-play further by using teacher-in-role or playwright-on-the-edge. You could use a scenario where the locals refuse to work in a Wacky Soap factory. Through active role-play, you can explore the relationships between workers drafted in from elsewhere and workers from the local community. There may be a small number of locals who do choose to accept a job at the factory.

Workers' delegation

A delegation of workers (the majority of the class) arrive to see the management team (students or teacher-in-role) about anxieties over a colleague who is beginning to abuse Wacky Soap. They believe he is in danger of disappearing and causing an accident at work due to an increasing deficit of limbs!

>> What is the responsibility of the management team?
>> Should the colleague be sacked or assisted by the company?
>> Should the contracts be written in such a way as to imply a specific management attitude to the workforce's use of wacky soap? If so, what are the wider implications of this?

These questions should be fed into the role-play by the teacher, either in-role or as playwright-on-the-edge, freezing the action and developing the story from the sidelines.

News item

A media figure (such as a pop star, footballer, MP or member of the royal family) has disappeared. The reason for their disappearance is claimed to be Wacky Soap abuse. Students should devise and present a two-minute news item which reports this story, including:

>> Information about the celebrity, and his/her battle with Wacky Soap
>> Interviews with family/friends
>> Interviews with Action Against Wacky Soap, the Wacky Soap Users Group and Wacky Soap Inc..

Wacky Soap script

You could also look at an extract from the original script. I have chosen one section (included at the end of the scheme – see page 20) which is ideal for whole-class presentation, with direction from the teacher. If all classes in one year group are working on *Wacky Soap* simultaneously (as they do in our school) then each group could work on a short section of the play to be shown in assembly, allowing all students to see much of the play episodically; this will generate more enthusiasm for the project.

Playwright-on-the-edge: the teacher takes on the role of playwright, holding up the action, focusing on important moments, or allowing them to be re-run if desired. PotE can slow down the action and ensure all participants are playing by the rules.

There are obvious real-life parallels you could draw to provoke further discussion.

Extracts should be presented in chronological order, so classes presenting earlier sections of the story should start working on their script extracts first.

There are other sections in the play which you could look at which would also be suitable for small group work and contain a lot of humour.

Whole-school production

The final extension activity is to put on a whole school production of the full musical, *Wacky Soap*. It has certainly gone down a treat whenever we have presented it in our school, and if all students at KS3 have worked on it at some stage, it will be a very popular production.

An extract from *Wacky Soap*
by Mark Wheeller

Storyteller: By one minute to one on the appointed day a large crowd gathered around the market square, each one clutching their rubber duck ...

All: and feeling really silly!

Storyteller: No-one could work out what had made King Huff decide to show himself after these three years.

Half everyday folk: I wonder why King Huff wants to see us today.

Other half: We can't work it out! Can you?

First half: No! We can't work it out either!

Storyteller: Finally the big clock in the market-place struck one. (It does so.)

All: *(To Storyteller)* Well? Where is King Huff then?

Storyteller: He's behind you!

Skunk: He must be on his own then.

All: Why's that?

Skunk: I can't smell his Mrs. *(They all laugh)*

Storyteller: She's here as well!

All: She can't be!

Storyteller: She is!

All: *(They look the wrong way.)* Where?

Storyteller: There!

All: Where?

Storyteller: There!

All: Oh no she's not.

Storyteller: *(Encouraging the audience to participate)* Oh yes she is!

All: Oh no she's not.

Storyteller: *(Encouraging the audience to participate)* Oh yes she is!

All: *(Seeing him)* Oh yes she is!

King: You seem surprised to see your King.

All: It's been three long years without hearing a thing!

Skunk: And we couldn't smell your Mrs. *(Everyone tries to shut Skunk up)*

King: I, my sweet smelling wife and my glamorous daughter ... have so much to tell.
But first I must ask ... how are you? Are you well?

Tom: Things are much the same for us Sirrah.

Storyteller: King Huff took this to mean that his subjects were unhappy.

King: All of you will be delighted to hear ...
That sadness you need no more fear.

Storyteller: His subjects looked surprised ... *(they do so)* ... and then worried ... *(they do so)*.

▶

King: A secure and happy ending, until now just a hope, is unequivocally ours, for I have invented this ... and I call it ... *(he holds a bar of Wacky Soap aloft)* ... Wacky Soap!

All: We don't want a happy ending.

Storyteller: Oh yes you do!

Tom: Shut up Storyteller!

King: *(To the Storyteller)* You've made me forget what I was going to ...

Think: What is this wacky soap? What does it do?

King: It will, I promise, work wonders for you!
It cleans away both dirt and discontent.

Queen: ... and leaves you clean and radient *(sic)*!

Skunk: Is this what stopped your Mrs from smelling?

Storyteller: The everyday folk of the Bower of Bliss looked at one another silently. No-one dared to say anything.

(A moment of uncomfortable silence.)

Queen: Yes. And I shall never smell, burp or pass wind again! Give King Huff a clap ... give him a cheer! *(Queen and Symbol clap and cheer enthusiastically but no-one else joins in)* So ... are you going to try the soap?

Skunk: If it stopped her from smelling it must be worth a go.

Tom: But apart from you Skunk ... we don't smell!

Junk: And we're all really wacky!

All: Look! *(They all pull wacky faces and dance and do other wacky stuff!)*

The Inks: We all live in picturesque cottages.

All: Three or four bedrooms ... each.

Pink: We all have beautiful children.

Punk: Well mannered.

All: Perfectly behaved!

Harriet: We all have lovely cars.

Junk: Digital TVs!

Tom: *(Picking a phone out of the buggy)* ... mobile phones!

Kink: And bright yellow bananas.

All: What?

Kink: Sometimes they're a bit brown ... but not very often!

All: King Huff ... we speak as one! We're wacky enough. We do not need your soap!

Tom: We use shamay.

Harriet: That's why we all look so young and beautiful.

All: We don't need your soap!

Queen: Shut up! Shut up!

(Silence)

Storyteller: The silence that fell on the market square was broken only moments later by the delicate footsteps of the adorable Princess Symbol walking towards the crowd. She stood confidently in front of the royal microphone. The crowd gasped as they heard for the first time the sweetness of her royal voice.

Symbol: I, like you, used shamay.
Now, I've learnt the Wacky Soap way.

Courtier: *(Clutching two bars of shamay)* Would you swap these two bars of ordinary shamay for one of your Wacky Soap bars?

Symbol: Certainly not! I'll always use Wacky Soap from now on.

(The everyday folk vomit in unison [mimed!])

I would like to thank dbda for allowing us to quote so freely from the script. If you would like to purchase a complete set of *Wacky Soap* resources, consisting of a full script, music score and mini musical, storybook and past performance CD, please contact dbda. Tel: 0870 333 7771, email: info@dbda.co.uk, address: Pin Point, 1–2 Rosslyn Crescent, Harrow, HA1 2SU. Quote code: WSSET

Playwriting

Introduction

Playwriting within my drama lessons is a recent development for me, brought on by two factors. Firstly, when I visit other schools I am becoming better known for my playwriting than my teaching so there is an expectation that I can 'teach' playwriting. Secondly my new role in the Academy where I teach allows me to undertake more interesting projects with groups of students who wish to pursue a specific interest i.e. playwriting.

Most of my work with young playwrights historically came within my role as youth theatre director; being a working playwright tends to attract young people wanting to have a go themselves to join the group. I often find I am not teaching playwriting so much as responding to students' self-taught efforts.

An excellent book on this subject is *Teaching Young Playwrights*, Gerald Chapman (foreword by Dorothy Heathcote) (1990, Heinemann).

I have, however, introduced a small amount of playwriting into our KS3 curriculum and have been delighted with how it's been received. I always like to gear playwriting towards being performed. The original idea for this scheme came from a workshop I attended many years ago.

Beyond this unit, our drama department practises a number of exercises to encourage students to develop more imaginative and stylistically devised work. Although these lessons don't necessarily involve any actual writing as such, I would argue that this does teach playwriting and hope that these skills will be applied when they come to write a play. When students come to write their first work, they often need a nudge to use these more imaginative ideas, as they tend to fall back on the most obvious ways of structuring dialogue. Although, once nudged, they don't look back!

A while ago, inspired by Channel 4's programme *The Play's the Thing*, I ran a playwriting competition across Year 8 that proved tremendously successful and raised the profile of playwriting in our school. Also, as it happened on a peripatetic basis, it did not eat into valuable curriculum drama lesson time. For those who might be interested in doing something similar, the structure of this was as follows:

The first two phases of the competition spanned from September to Christmas.

>> All students in Year 8 submit a proposal of a synopsis for a five-minute play (two to four characters), written in an English lesson. The English teacher of each group reads all of these and selects two or three from each class to go forward to the second round of the competition – the workshop phase.

>> The selected students are extracted from their regular lessons for an hour a week to participate in a series of classroom-based playwriting workshops.

>> During the Christmas holidays, students either devised their ideas from their original submission or started again on their synopsis. They were aiming to write a five-minute play.

>> By the time they returned in January, they had all made a start, though it has to be said that some dropped out at this point. We spent each lesson reading through some of the plays, offering feedback and suggestions. This feedback aimed to be useful for all playwrights, but would be specific to each individual.

>> While listening to the ideas of other playwrights helped each student to develop their work, hearing their own play being read out loud offered them an opportunity to find out if the pace was appropriate, if words were repeated, or if a character had over-long periods with nothing to do. Students always left workshop lessons with new ideas to develop or to re-draft their play.

>> By the beginning of the Easter holidays, the completed five-minute scripts were all handed in. My job over the holidays was to select six plays that would progress to a final performance.

>> Following the Easter break, the winners were announced and each student had the opportunity to cast their play from their year group.

>> The cast and director were to meet during the peripatetic hour to rehearse. In the end, this turned out to be impossible due to my exam commitments and the use of our rehearsal space, so we arranged a whole day towards the end of June when all performers and directors rehearsed in the morning for four hours, and performed to the rest of their year group in the afternoon.

>> We decided not to make the final performances competitive, thus not have one final winner. Instead, all six chosen playwrights were invited on a free theatre trip as their prize, which proved an incredibly effective way of highlighting the work of the playwrights and raised the confidence of a small number of students who began to see themselves as writers.

In our school, I ran about ten of these workshops. The material came largely from Gerald Chapman's book (and some others listed at the end of this scheme), together with exercises I developed myself.

Throughout this unit, I refer to students as playwrights as it raises their status.

I allowed the students to cast and direct their own play to create a sense of pride.

Playwriting

The scheme

What follows is a series of ideas for lessons. I recommend using them not as a scheme of work but rather as something to dip into.

Session 1

Resources:
A handout or projection, comparing a page from a novel and a page from a play script.

This session works best in a classroom with chairs and desks.

Learning objective

To teach the conventions of a play script layout.

Start the lesson by showing the class a page of a novel together with a page of a typical play script. Ask them to say what the obvious differences between the two pages are. Point out key elements of layout and highlight salient points, such as:

>> The characters' name in the margin
>> Stage directions in brackets and italics
>> An increased number of words consisting of one syllable, which adds pace to the speech.

Collaborative playwriting

A lot of the lines are very short. Many students will assume that long lines are more meritorious – I mention that shorter lines make for a faster script.

This exercise encourages weaker writers to feel more comfortable, particularly as it endorses short lines for injecting pace into a scene. Explain that, for this play script, you want students to only write what the characters say, even though there are plays where inner thoughts are revealed.

This could be done on a laptop and projected onto a screen.

Issue each student with a sheet of margined A4 paper. Ask them to write their own name at the top right hand corner of the page. Inform the class that you will participate in this exercise and initiate a short discussion to establish the following points:

>> Location – where is the play to be set? Once decided, this can be written on the top line of the paper.
>> What shall the two characters in this play be called? Try to establish unisex names. Once decided, the two names should be written on the second and third line of the paper.

>> As a group, decide on an opening line. Ask for suggestions and discuss their various merits. Once decided, allocate this line to one of the names. Write that name in the margin and the spoken line on the other side of the margin.

Tell students that they will invent and write on their sheet the second character's reply to the opening line, followed by the first character's response to that, and finally the second character's response to the first character's second line. Before they pick up their pens, remind students that they will need to use these lines to establish certain things in the script:

>> Names of characters and possibly their relationship with each other (or lack of it)
>> Location, or at least the atmosphere it engenders
>> An idea of what might happen (setting an expectation which may or may not be fulfilled).

I also tell students to:
>> Avoid going round in circles – each line should help the story to progress
>> Each response must make sense, but doesn't have to be very long.

After they have completed their lines, ask students to put their pens down to await the next instruction, as the session is to go in an unexpected direction: tell them to swap their script with someone else.

Once students have the new script in front of them, ask them to read the opening three lines and invent an appropriate fourth line, which is to be said by the character that didn't say the previous line. Once completed, students swap their scripts again with someone else, read that student's script and continue as before by adding the next line for the appropriate character. Students should swap their scripts with whoever is ready and with as many different people as possible. Allow the swapping to go on until most of the scripts have filled two thirds of the first page, then ask for the sheets to be returned to the originator (whose name is at the top of the sheet).

I have encountered a list of problems at this point, which I usually point out to the class before the exercise starts – once all the warnings are issued, students can start swapping their scripts:

>> Students lose track of who is who and allocate lines to the 'wrong' character
>> Students write exactly the same line on the different scripts they receive
>> Swearing appears
>> Sections of the script do not make sense.

Due to time constraints, I sometimes pre-plan both location (for example, a graveyard or a haunted house – both popular settings from my experience) and names. However, allowing the group to generate this information creates a sense of ownership, which teacher decisions can never achieve as effectively.

This structure offers the originator no control over the progress of the first part of the scene, thus they are compelled to be open to developments and possibilities that they wouldn't initially have considered.

It is always a good idea to set up a mystery to provide motivation for completing a task quickly.

I generally use my role as writer to put in unexpected plot developments; the wackier the better – it evokes more imaginative responses.

Only if any of the above occurs, does the current writer have my permission to alter the script. If students are completely confused by what they have in front of them, ask them to swap scripts with you and then you can make the necessary changes. At no stage should anyone make an alteration purely on the basis of disliking what is written down.

The originator should read the scripts (and, if appropriate, make any corrections) and continue the play (at least to the end of the second A4 side), giving it either a conclusion or a cliff-hanger ending.

At the end of the session, collect all scripts, then select just over half of them and photocopy them in preparation for the next session.

Session 2

Ask the class to pair up.

Issue two copies of one of the scripts selected in the previous lesson to each pair, and explain that their task is to find a way of presenting the script to an audience.

Stress that the action of the play may well begin prior to the first line being spoken, and serves to set the scene.

Each group has 25 minutes to devise a staging of the scene and to learn the lines. Even though students will baulk at this, for most of them it will not (to their surprise) cause problems.

The final section of this session (and probably the one after) is reserved for presentations of the various plays. Prior to each performance, say the name of the originating playwright, for example 'thanks to x and y for performing z's play.'

Mark the performers in the following way:

Four marks for cooperation during the rehearsals

Two marks for word-learning

Two marks for appropriate use of movement (making it look real)

Two marks for interpretation of the duologue (making it sound real).

Stress that writing is never completely finished and that there are always changes to be made on scripts, which continue to undergo development no matter how finished they appear to be. Some playwrights will think they are finished after their first draft, be it an improvisation or a written piece. The following exercises put the emphasis on the value of re-writing to change and develop their efforts.

Creative (re-)writing

This is a great quick starter for a session:

>> Write down one fact about yourself

>> Develop this fact by exaggeration – add some factors that are not true

>> Write down the same fact, but this time make it rhyme

>> Write it down again, but add something unexpected or unusual.

Now ...

>> Write a paragraph about anything you want. Don't chew over it, in a few minutes you will be re-writing it

>> Now re-write it in fewer words

>> Re-write again, but this time using more words and more flowery language.

I used all of these ideas in the playwriting workshops for my version of *The Play's the Thing* competition.

When playwrights first write that paragraph, they are flying blind, yet when they re-write it, they experience how every draft informs and enlightens subsequent drafts.

Fantasy letters

This idea stems from Gerald Chapman's excellent book and encourages the two characters to have different 'voices'.

Divide the class into pairs and let them sit next to one another. As pairs mustn't talk, they can only communicate through the medium of a letter, which should be based on the following children's rhyme:

> **Hey diddle diddle,**
>
> The cat and the fiddle,
>
> The cow jumped over the moon.
>
> The little dog laughed to see such fun
>
> And the dish ran away with spoon.

One playwright plays the role of the little dog. The little dog writes a letter to the spoon asking why he or she has run away with the dish, and whether there's any chance of returning to the fork with whom the spoon used to be very happy. The other playwright plays the spoon and refuses to return, but has to give reasons for this refusal (and perhaps reasons as to why he or she ran away with the dish). Playwrights swap roles, with the playwright writing as the spoon always offering different reasons for their refusal to return, until you are satisfied that they have worked hard enough.

The letters then need to be translated into a duologue.

Rule: Playwrights can only use the words that were used in the letters. Tell playwrights that the scripts are going to be performed by another pair, so someone else needs to be able to understand what they have written. Playwrights should ensure that their writing communicates their intention. It is important that during the rehearsals, improvements can continue to be made to the script.

Finally, swap the scripts so that playwrights can read through their new script. In the next session, they will perform a script they did not write.

Unspoken words

Introduce the next activity by asking playwrights to listen to friends and to how they sometimes don't finish their sentences, using filler words such as 'well', 'like' or 'err' instead. Also ask them to pay attention to how often they repeat themselves, and whether this moves the conversation forward or makes it go round in circles.

> Write a scene involving a brother and sister: one is trying to reveal to the other that either they or their girlfriend have/has fallen pregnant. However, this is only revealed in the very last line. Making extensive use of broken sentences and filler words gives a tension to the scene; the audience knows that one character is trying to reveal information but cannot find a way of doing so.

Once again, it is a good idea to get two actors to perform the script to check that the playwrights have successfully communicated their intentions through the written words.

Developing characters

Explain that it often helps to know the people you are writing about, even if they are not in the context from which you know them.

Ask the playwrights the following questions:

>> If you were going to write a play about someone you know, who would you choose and why?
>> Come up with two people who could provide you with inspiration for a play.
>> Now try placing them as characters in a story you know, for example *Little Red Riding Hood*. Who would they be?

Ask playwrights to write a scene or speech from *Little Red Riding Hood* using real-life characters to inspire the fiction characters' words/actions.

This activity first appeared in the Schoolplay Productions book *Sweet FA* (teachers' notes) by Mark Wheeller and Ginny Spooner – www.schoolplayproductions.co.uk

> ## TWO-TOUCH THEATRE
>
> I developed this from a football training game I enjoyed as a child, in which the player is only allowed to touch the ball once or twice. While the first touch can control, the second one has to pass, shoot or clear the ball. If a third consecutive touch is made, a free kick is awarded to the opposition. A football coach would use this game to ensure that all players have a good opportunity to get involved, to speed up the game and to make the players think quickly.
>
> In two-touch theatre, each actor can only use one or two words. Actors must not share sentences between characters. It is an exercise in précis and an effective way of communicating a lot of information quickly. A two-touch scene can announce a location (third line of the scene underneath), announce feelings (first and fourth line), speak to others in the group (all remaining lines) or clarify a mimed action (dual-purpose last line).

A:	(*Relaxing.*)	A:	Problem?
B:	(*Searching.*)	B:	My kangaroo.
A:	Peaceful Park.	A:	Kangaroo?
B:	(*Panics, trips over A.*)	B:	Lost.
A:	You all right?	A:	(*Pointing.*) Over there!
B:	No!	B:	(*Giving A a wad of notes.*) Huge reward!

To learn the technique, I ask actors to create a two-touch scene using the following story:

> Setting: A bank.
>
> *(Establish a run-of-the-mill bank scene with customers and clerks.)*
>
> The scene gets interrupted by the arrival of two robbers. *(As a pair, they can only use a maximum of two words, meaning they count as one character. Alternatively, they could speak chorally.)* A brief cartoon-style comic fight follows *(as this involves only two actions and two reactions, make sure to select actions that will enhance the scene.)*
>
> Money is handed over by a clerk. Just as the robbers are about to leave, a superhero 'flies' in (it's always interesting to see how this is staged) and rescues the situation. The scene ends with all except the robbers and the superhero saying chorally: 'my hero'.

I outline the story so that actors are focused on using the two-touch limitation, rather than inventing a story.

When learning this technique, be rigid with the rules, except for when applying it to an improvisation. Only use this technique when and where appropriate.

I include here an example of this style of theatre. Where a line should have some added significance, I wrote them out to contrast with the other lines. I felt this was a particularly effective scene, and when staged can be very powerful.

Sue:	Then the arguments started …
Corey:	*(Arguing, stating the lines in the style described above, building to a climax.)* Ongoing …
Sue:	Taking up from the last time …
Corey:	… Bringing stuff up from the past …
Sue:	… Clutching at straws …
Corey:	… Lying …
Sue:	… Suspecting …
Corey:	… But not proving …
Sue:	… Not being able to prove anything …
Corey:	… Provoking …
Sue:	… Feeling frustrated …
Corey:	… Defensive …
Sue:	… Attacking …
Corey:	… Shouting …
Sue:	… Louder …
Corey:	… Hurtful …
Sue:	… Passionate …
Corey:	… Swearing …
Sue:	… What has happened to you?
Corey:	… Bad swearing … can't believe I'm saying this to my mum … really bad swearing.
Sue:	… We didn't bring you up like this, Corey!
Corey:	… Tearful …
Sue:	… Out of control …
Corey:	… Raising hands …
Sue:	… Fists …
Both:	Fighting!
Corey:	Then dad got involved.
Mike:	*(To Sue.)* Why?
Sue:	*(Referring to Corey.)* It's her.
Mike:	Why?
Corey:	*(Referring to Sue.)* It's her.
Corey/Sue:	Fighting! ▶

The Gate Escape by Mark Wheeller (dbda 2004) is used here with permission.

Mike:	Why?
Corey/Sue:	*(To each other.)* It's her!
Mike:	*(Shouts.)* If you don't stop ... I'm out of here! *(Silence)*
Sue:	Corey, we can't go on like this ...
Corey:	Well, stop going on at me then!
Sue/Mike:	Can't you see ... you're wasting your life?
Corey:	*(Turning in slow motion to the audience to say this line passionately.)* I'd hate it if I had to live life like you want me to.

Developing plays from oral testimony

One approach that supports new playwrights is to use oral testimony. In my experience, frameworks like this often lead groups of actors into more imaginative/theatrical work. Tell actors to create a play script without using any words other than those in the text below (and, if necessary, simple linking words). If they are being used in conversation, phrases can be put in the present tense.

A good starting point is to highlight phrases that you think may be selected to go into the play, then consider how to put them in order (it can be interesting to play around with the chronology) or juxtapose them.

The advantage of this way of working, particularly for actors who may not be confident writers, is that it gives you a sense of confidence to use words you know are correct.

Ali's story

The following is taken from the testimony of a reformed truant from Basingstoke I interviewed in my preparation for the play *The Gate Escape*. Ali was one of the people whose words I used in the play. It is a story students will relate to well as it tells of a girl looking back on this troubled period of her life (at the age the reader is) from the perspective of being a little, but not much, older.

My reports said how it would be much better if I was in school more. I'd be in about two days but not go to all the lessons. We used to get away with it ... but now ... they're like, 'Who's out of school? Who's missing?' Ours were always the first names. I've changed the game now... it's more exciting to prove them wrong ... to prove that we are not the ones who are out there.

My life at home is better now ... I've started to live with my Nan cos we got kicked out of our house ... my whole family got kicked out ... cos Mum didn't pay any rent ... plus my mum's got so many letters warning of taking her to court when I didn't go to school.

'Please go to school. I haven't got the money to pay for a fine for you.'

'Mum I don't like school!'

'No-one likes school ... but you just have to go and learn.'

'Well I don't listen when I'm there anyway.'

'Well you have to!'

'I don't like Miss Dobson. She picks on me.'   ▶

I used to blame most of it on her.

Cos I'd missed so much school I felt really thick cos everyone was like ... "Oh I know the answer to this" ... I was just sat there in the corner and getting back to be friends with everyone ... they realised that I was trying to sort my life out, blah blah blah. I hated being on the outside ... I used to carve stuff on my arms cos I hated it so much ... I wrote 'I hate life' on my arm. Now I'm at school I get on with people so much better ... at junior school I was really popular ... then it went really down ... all the girls were really scared of me.

I have caught up a bit ... I know I've got to be in school and get my grades - it's only two terms really ... I mean I've caught up pretty well.

People'd say: "Why do you bunk?" "It's good fun ... going into town with your mates." "Yeh but you might as well just stay in school, you can do exactly the same." "Yeh I suppose but I just like going out of school."

But it's the look on their face, the way they think they're better than me. I'm not saying that I'm all goodie-goodie still ... but at the end of the day I want to get good grades to prove my mum wrong ... my sister was really bright but she started to bunk as well in Yr 11 to be with her boyfriend. I swear that if I get like her then I need to be shot!

I do hairdressing at the moment ... so cos I've got my level one already I'm going to do my level two & three in hairdressing after school so that's what I'm planning to do ... I'd like my own business.

I'm actually ashamed of my past, even though it was my choice to do it ... but ... I just wish ... I wouldn't want to start over again, there's too much time.

Further reading

Teaching Young Playwrights, Gerald Chapman (foreword Dorothy Heathcote) (1990, Heinemann)

Can We Write It as a Play? Barry Simner (1994, Hodder Arnold H&S)

The Young Playwrights Page, a website created by Jon Dorf, where you will also find details of his excellent book *Young Playwrights 101*. www.jondorf.com/youngplaywrights

Warden X

Introduction

This scheme of work serves as a high impact opener to the use of teacher-in-role. It is set in a young offenders' institution or borstal. The scheme is based on an idea by Dorothy Heathcote, witnessed at the Cockpit Theatre, London, in the early 1980s. You can imagine how excited I was to actually witness Dorothy teaching, after hearing so much about her while I was at Stantonbury. For me it was like seeing George Best or David Bowie ... I was watching one of my idols!

I always cite this as the best drama lesson I have ever seen (or done) and probably will ever see. At the workshop, Dorothy was very down-to-earth; I think she was carrying a shopping bag when she walked in. None of the participants had rehearsed although the structuring of their improvisation was very cleverly managed. I believe the group on show was a non-option Year 9 group from a local school who had virtually no experience of drama. They were obviously nervous when they emerged onto stage in front of a sell-out audience, yet with Dorothy's magical guidance they presented a play which gripped the audience, leaving us on the edge of our seats. This was theatre at its very best, even though it was 'only' a spontaneous improvisation.

I have delivered this scheme and continued to develop it every year since that day. It remains a scheme I know will win over any difficult class. I have used it in the first term of every new job I have had with all my Year 9 classes (traditionally the most difficult groups). It is regularly highlighted by outgoing Year 11s as their favourite scheme of work from lower-school drama.

I think teacher-in-role lessons have gained a reputation of being little more than discussions. Warden X is very clearly an action drama; the relationship between the teacher-in-role and the students-in-role is incredibly highly-charged. There is virtually no seated discussion. The ongoing story is action-based and has an intriguing whodunit plot.

The scheme

Section 1

Setting the scene

Initiate this part by asking the class to tell you what they know about young offenders'
institutions (YOI) or borstals. Aim to establish who would be there and why, and discuss the
basics of their daily routine.

I briefly introduce what these institutions were like when I was a boy in the 1960s. In those
days the name I would have used was borstal. These were much more military than YOIs.
The regime was tough and there were cases where some wardens allegedly showed little (or
no) kindness to the detainees they were in charge of. Take care that this introduction does
not slow the pace down to the extent that you lose interest from the outset.

>> Once the picture of this institution is built up, ask the class to prepare a scene depicting
utter normality; nothing exciting should be happening. This scene is set during the
final two minutes of the last half hour of the evening. Say that this is part of the borstal's
daily routine. The timetabled activity is social time, a moment of normality in this
otherwise harsh regime.

>> Activities during this time must be confined to one room specifically set up for social
activities. This room has seats, pool tables, and table tennis tables, but no television
or computer games. The whole class should make plans (give them five minutes) to
depict the final two minutes of this social time prior to the warden coming to take the
roll call.

>> Students should work as a whole group but can choose how they sub-group.
They should find their own space in the room in which to rehearse their activity.

>> All students will need to have a chair, even if they are not using it during the
prepared scene.

>> Stress that their activities should be active (even if it is a (mimed) game of cards) and
should be mundane. Students are allowed to converse, but these conversations should
be consciously everyday.

>> Once they've planned their two-minute scene, ask them all to run it through
simultaneously, without anyone watching. Explain that you are only watching to see
that they are concentrating and staying in role. You are not, at this point, concerned
about content other than it should be mundane. This activity is a means to an end, not
an end in itself.

>> I am very strict about what I expect and will not move on to Section 2 (which I say is where the drama begins) until everyone is able to do this simple task with complete concentration and commitment.

>> Each group should be able to repeat their presentation and aim *not* to add embellishments to the scene.

Section 2

NUMBERING

Ask for a volunteer to number everyone in the class, leaving one number spare. If there are 24 in the class there will be 25 numbers, one number (preferably not number 1) not belonging to anyone.

It is best that the numbering is done without you knowing which number matches which person or which number is spare. Each of the class will need to know their own number and the spare number.

Teacher-in-role

Introduce the role you are to be playing: the most hated warden in the institution. You can elaborate on this as much as you want, but it is important to stress that all the young offenders are scared of this warden.

It is helpful to offer a short example of how reactions assist a performer. Ask the volunteer to land a punch towards your stomach but stopping (crucially) just before it hits. The volunteer is instructed to do this twice in as similar a manner as possible. To the first, make no reaction. To the second, react as though you have had a hard blow to the stomach. This illustrates clearly how important reacting is. In the same way, Warden X cannot be scary unless the prisoners play scared. However, remember that, equally importantly, students should not overplay this fear.

Explain that, now they have prepared their two minutes of the social time, the drama is ready to unfold. This time Warden X will enter. This should trigger students to move to their chairs, all the time watching Warden X.

>> The class replay the final two minutes of the social time (above), only this time you will enter as Warden X. Indicate Warden X's entrance by banging the door of the studio. As soon as that happens everyone moves to stand in front of their seat ensuring that they are facing the door/Warden X. There will be a period of (dramatic) silence. All await their instruction (from Warden X) to sit down. No more than this is planned. Do not even tell them that Warden X will conduct a roll call.

>> From this point on, the drama becomes a genuinely spontaneous improvisation, although you will have markers that you are looking for to steer the story.

>> Having entered as Warden X, I sometimes go straight into calling the register by number but more often I walk across the space and introduce my role by speaking a third person narration:

> Warden X looked around him (*does so*). There seemed to be an unnatural silence that evening. Something was different. The warden did not know why but he was sure ... something was different.

Then, as Warden X, call out the register.

> Warden: '1?'
>
> Number 1: 'Here.'
>
> Warden: (*now shouting to correct the student*) 'Sir! Here, sir!'
>
> Number 1: 'Here sir!'

Warden X takes the opportunity of leading the roll call to demonstrate their character.

The register-taking should be interrupted on suitable occasions by teacher-in-role narrating (in the third person) as a voice over:

> Warden X noted the look that passed between numbers 4 and 5 (for example) but still couldn't put his finger on what might have made this happen.

This narration should aim to heighten the tension as to what will happen when you call out the unallocated number. When the number is called you should, in role, cross-question anyone who has drawn your attention to them already in the roll call or, failing that, the two numbers either side of the unallocated one. Establish where prisoner 15 would normally sit and who, if anyone, they would normally sit next to (for the purposes of this article the unallocated number was 15). It's best to avoid giving prisoner 15 a gender (refer to them just as '15').

These questions should be kept brief as you do not want detailed answers at this point. The class should be sufficiently thrown by the questions so that the authority of your role allows you to move at your own pace through the answers.

Once the roll call is completed the questioning can resume for a short while. The tone of the questioning should be threatening and bullying, always demanding that you are called 'Sir', 'Ma'am' or 'Warden X' at the end of every response.

Take the opportunity to ask individuals to get their coats and go and look in the toilets, the gym and (significantly) the boiler room. Narrate them to the point where they each return with the news that they have found nothing. Then play through the conversations that reveal their lack of discoveries.

At the end of this session, ask the inmates to line up in number order without talking. They should stand with their hands behind their back all facing in the same direction.

You should take every opportunity to have a pop at any of the young offenders, such as demanding that they answer in a formal manner; this should continue so that each sentence they speak ends with the warden's name or title. There is also the opportunity for some use of sarcasm to promote the warden's cruel streak.

Do not allow the class to try to solve the problem of where prisoner 15 is. If this begins to happen, interrupt and move the action on.

N.B. The students don't go to the real gym etc. They step out of the drama for the time it would take them to get there and back.

Standing in front of them, say something along the lines of:

> 'I am determined to get to the bottom of this. Prisoner 15 will be found. How dare this happen on my duty! I am sure that there are those among you who have something to say but are scared to do so. You should bear in mind though that some of you are coming up for parole and will not want this event to jeopardise your chances.
>
> 'I shall offer you all the opportunity to talk to me in private. I would like you to indicate to me whether you have something you wish to tell me by clenching your fist as I pass behind you and tap you lightly on the shoulder.'

I would choose to eyeball individuals as I say this, giving them a clue that they may be about to be released on parole.

Warden X walks along behind the group tapping each on the shoulder. Normally only a handful will clench their fists. I always lie, saying:

> 'Interesting. Do you know, over half of you are prepared to say something to me in private. If that is the case I believe that most, if not all of you, will have something to report. Bearing this in mind, I shall repeat my walk along your line to see if any more of you wish to speak out. Perhaps you were afraid to do so the first time. However, now you know you are not alone. Remember, if you choose to keep quiet and it is later established that you knew something you could end up in serious trouble.'

As a result of this, students won't know whether to believe each other and any conversation about their reactions is rendered pointless.

Warden X then walks and repeats the exercise. Normally some who did not clench their fist the first time round will do so this time. Before you dismiss the class, tell them not to reveal whether they clenched their fists in any out-of-role conversations they may have. Thus the seed is sown that they should mislead each other (in their out-of-role conversations between lessons) about what they did to make the improvisation game more exciting. This normally generates much discussion as they leave the lesson.

Session 3

Discussion

Prisoner 15 should remain of unspecified gender.

>> Recap the story so far. Encourage comments on character, with particular reference to Warden X and prisoner 15 (the victim). Explain that the scene they worked on in the previous lesson would chronologically appear towards the end of the story we are working on. Our task now is to go back in time to see what led to this scene; more particularly why no-one would speak out and say where prisoner 15 is or was. What could have happened to him/her? I sometimes say that I know prisoner 15 looked upon themselves as a victim in the social group they were forced to be in.

>> Discuss the concept of a victim. Think of examples from real life and famous films or television programmes. Why are we interested in victims' stories?

>> Divide the class into groups of four, five or six. Each group should develop a series of tableaux to show what kind of back story could have led prisoner 15 to be outcast. What has made prisoner 15 a victim?

>> This will throw up lots of ideas about what makes a victim and what could have happened to prisoner 15. The problem is how to decide which one to go with. This decision will be deferred until later.

THE FIGHT IN THE BOILER ROOM

Ask the students to explain what a boiler room is. Do they know where the one in their school is? What is in there?

This is where the fight occurs, which leads to the death/injury of prisoner 15. No wardens are in earshot. There is no CCTV in there.

The fight between prisoner 15 and another inmate is pre-planned. It will be in the style of a sound-only radio presentation.

The group get into a rough circle. Place a coat in the centre of the circle to represent the immobile body of prisoner 15. The teacher squats down towards the inner edge of the circle, ready to cue various moments of the action.

The activity will be noisy and is initiated by the chant: 'Fight, fight, fight'.

The fight is built up by carefully-directed rehearsal. The process may be slow but I always rehearse it as a class activity from the outset, as it can be helpful with difficult classes. The students may need lots of help to arrive at a sound picture and many may naturally want to move (physically) to make the sound seem more natural. This is fine, but the fight must not actually happen. Their moves have to be the moves of those watching the fight. The fight itself must remain in the mind's eye and be created by the noise around it.

The use of atmospheric lights (and spotlight on the coat) is a helpful addition to this piece of work.

The three cues I use, following the initial chant of 'fight, fight, fight', are:

1. The start of the fight.
2. The moment the aggressor (not prisoner 15) draws a knife The reaction to this must be carefully portrayed. Some will support it, some will not be too happy about it and may begin to sympathise with prisoner 15 – most of them secretly, but some openly. Others will carry on regardless, sure that no harm will be done.
3. The moment prisoner 15 is struck down by a knife blow.

1. Demonstrate a rolling hands motif to cue the class in.

2. Demonstrate in an exaggerated manner a knife being pulled from a pocket. Leave hand in the air.

3. Move your hand down as though holding the knife.

This cue denotes the end of the scene and complete silence from everyone should follow.

When you feel everyone is making it seem realistic go for a 'take'. The only difference with the take is that the students will find out with whom prisoner 15 had the fight. They will be revealed by choosing to move forward and stand next to the coat. Often, more than one person wants to take on this role. If this is the case then you could wait in silence while all but one person step aside and if this doesn't seem likely to happen, question the volunteers as to why they were fighting prisoner 15, then either allow the class to choose which person to go with, choose yourself, or find a way of randomly selecting who it should be. Do not allow this to be pre-planned, as it is better to make full use of the added tension of surprise.

Once selected, mark the moment by asking each person watching the fight (except the aggressor), in turn, to state the moment which stood out for them. For example:
>> 'Some blood splashed on my boot'
>> 'I remember the sound of a bucket being knocked over'.

Remind the class that you know from the roll call scene that no one tells Warden X later that evening about the fight.

There must have been a few people here who were on prisoner 15's side. Identify them simply by asking who would like to take on that role. There can be two or three (a boyfriend/ girlfriend is always a good role for someone to adopt). What happened between this moment and the roll call to stop anyone from speaking out?

It is the task of the aggressor to ensure that no one leaves the boiler room until:

>> The body (which may not be dead) of prisoner 15 is disposed of (hidden or destroyed)
>> Evidence is disposed of/cleaned within the confines of the boiler room (who actually helps with this?)
>> A firm commitment is secured from everyone not to say anything.

It is also important to stress that this scene cannot go on forever. Often by this time it is nearly the end of the lesson.

Tell the group that some people should give the aggressor a hard time but that they will need support from others in order that the resolution you know happens does actually occur. In other words, the group saying nothing to Warden X about where prisoner 15 is already in the subsequent roll call.

Then play through the fight scene (again, as a radio play) and move into an improvised action scene, which needs to be led by the person who has taken on the role of aggressor. The above bullet points are then performed.

This normally develops into a fantastic scene where you can play the role of playwright on the edge (PotE), orchestrating the scene and focusing on a particular line of conversation or action.

Session 3

The missing number needs to remain the same although due to absences and bad memories, everyone may need to be re-numbered.

Ask the class to replay the scene from Session 1 (the roll call scene). It won't be a bland replay but will be different because the group now have information about the non-appearance of prisoner 15 and will continue beyond the moment where it previously stopped. Knowing about the fight will make the scene different. For example, students will all know who the aggressor was. This should affect the way in which the teacher in role plays Warden X. I would choose to mention this person in one of my early narrations:

> 'Warden X noted how number 4 avoided eye contact and thought this to be strange.'
>
> or:
>
> 'Warden X noticed number 4 looking over at number 16. It made him/her wonder if number 16 had something to say.'
>
> Something else I have done during this scene is to come out of role, (becoming PotE) stopping the scene, and asking:
>
> I'd like to ask 4 to have a conversation with 16, which in real life they could never have had because Warden X is here. What would you say to number 16 knowing that they are the most likely person to let the cat out of the bag?

It is difficult to dictate what should happen from now on, as circumstances will be different each time. Replay all the main events so far: the prisoners who go to the gym; the toilets and the boiler room; and, of course, the line-up where students say whether they wish to speak privately to Warden X.

Go on, as Warden X, to conduct interviews in the middle of the class circle (Warden X's office) with those who offered to speak privately with Warden X.

To make these interviews more interesting, frame one of the other students who is most vocal in the lesson or upon whom you are able to impose a suitable motive. This can offer others a reason for spilling the truth.

Another idea is to make Warden X a 'bent' warden, who is prepared to spare the aggressor and is perhaps bribing the parent, or has a vendetta against another prisoner.

It is also possible to create an ending to this scene where Warden X reveals that they knew all along, thanks to the foresight of one of the prisoners, and that number 15 is now in hospital and will, we hope, make a full recovery. The prisoner who told is to be released on parole in return for having revealed the truth. Of course, the truth can be far from it. The prisoner being released could have framed another prisoner. Do any of the silent prisoners now speak up and, if so, how does Warden X deal with this?

Remind the students that, in the light of their role in the story, they may wish to alter their attitude to clenching their fists.

Optional extension activities

Various issues can be discussed:
1. How should the aggressor be dealt with?
2. What should happen to prisoner 15?
3. What should happen to the institution in which this event occurred?
4. What should happen to those on duty and the person in charge of the regime?
5. How will this incident be reported by the media?

4. This becomes a particularly interesting idea if some kind of back story can be created giving Warden X (in retrospect) a reason for framing one of the inmates.

Character work

It is interesting to look at the aggressor or Warden X and present a side of them which makes the audience care for them. A scene which might occur at some point prior to the time scale of the above story could be developed. It may well mean a subtle change needs to be made to the existing story, or adding something which was unseen in the scenes already shown.

Victims in plays

'A dramatist must examine the actions and motivation of even the most reprehensible characters and present them to us as people with whom we can connect. This means that we the audience, must care as much about the rapist as the victim; the torturer as the prey. We may be invited to make a judgement, but before we can do that we must understand. This is an uncomfortable but fundamental truth of all good drama. Good drama thrives on the messy complexity of life ... the best drama grows in that grey moral area where we are not sure who is 'right' and who is 'wrong'.

Can We Write it as a Play? Barry Simner (1994, Hodder Arnold H&S)

The Dome

Introduction

I have developed this scheme of work (which we use with Year 10 GCSE students but is equally good for older students) over many years. It is my favourite original scheme of work and works well with big classes of between 20 and 35. What follows is a summary of many of the ideas I have used when teaching this scheme. I have also successfully used edited versions of it on one-day courses. I would stress that the narrative is important and that anyone who wishes to shorten the scheme considers the pacing of the narrative carefully.

I would also suggest that you do not reveal too much of what the scheme is about so that a sense of the unknown surrounding the story is retained. The current trend of telling students what they are about to do in a lesson doesn't work in this instance! The surprise element will keep all participants more engaged as they will be motivated by the progression of the narrative. One of the great memories I have whenever I do this scheme is the (sometimes heated) debate that goes on as participants walk out of the classroom. They are often still discussing it many weeks later!

This work is developed from my understanding of Dorothy Heathcote's awe-inspiring style of working, one of which was to have whole classes dealing with overarching narratives. The idea that functioned as a catalyst for this more structured piece of work was developed by a group of Luke Abbott's students at Stantonbury. His simple starter was a hanged man rigged up in the drama studio. He followed this with questions to establish the location, which transpired to be a post-nuclear landscape. This in turn provided the stimulus for my development of these 'dome' sessions.

I remember doing the hanged man start-up a number of times when I started as a head of department in Epping, only I would set it in the post-nuclear world from the start. One day a student came up with an amazing anecdote. He claimed to live opposite the entrance to a nuclear shelter so he said he would be alright (if he was at home) when the siren went off. He would just walk over to the shelter and he'd be safe. I remember the class being up in arms about how unfair this would be and we talked about how people would get into the shelter. We supposed they would have to employ soldiers to stop people who weren't allowed in. Then the question arose: 'who would be allowed into the shelter?'.

In my next school, another anecdote surfaced which seemed to answer this question. A student claimed that his father had, many years previously, received a letter from the city council inviting him to take up a place in the Southampton nuclear shelter in the event of a nuclear war. I was somewhat sceptical about this and have not checked the authenticity of the claim ... the myth is fine by me! The letter allegedly stated that the place in the nuclear shelter was open to him but not to other members of his family. He was offered the place because of his high-ranking position in the city council. Later, this student's sister corroborated the story and another student whose father was a doctor said the same had happened to his dad. It set up an amazing concept: someone, somewhere would be dividing society into those who are important enough to be saved and those who are not.

What interested me as a playwright was how the unimportant people left to be killed by the nuclear blast would react to their treatment if they managed to survive the nuclear attack. More particularly, how would they react when the 'important people' emerged from the shelter? All I had to do was to contrive a situation where this could all be explored, by structuring a storyline.

In doing so, I had to invent certain things which are not scientifically accurate. I explain this to the participants, for example I tell them that for the purposes of this improvisation the shelter will offer 100 years of safety. I stress that these are my inventions for the purpose of this story and not scientific facts.

In both cases the students assured me that their respective parents had turned the offer down.

The Dome

Resources

Laptop/projector with countdown of 60 seconds

Pre-prepared letter inviting an individual to take up a place in the shelter and printed on headed notepaper

Sound effect of a siren (if this is not available, the teacher can merely say the word 'siren')

Film:

Threads (1984, BBC Film)

When the Wind Blows (1986, 4 DVD)

CDs:

War Requiem – Benjamin Britten

'Two Tribes' – Frankie goes to Hollywood (remix), which has someone reading out what to do in the event of a nuclear war and how to cope in a shelter

Suggested books:

Brother in the Land – Robert Swindells

Z for Zachariah – Robert O'Brien

When the Wind Blows – Raymond Briggs

The scheme

Scheme structure overview

1. Whole group tableau: the moments surrounding the closure of the nuclear shelter doors
2. Families or flatmates, one of whom holds a place in the shelter: small group spontaneous role-play leading to a public performance of the early stages of that improvisation. This leads to a whole class spontaneous improvisation with teacher as playwright-on-the-edge.
3. A scene outside the shelter prior to the bomb going off presented in a Brechtian narrative style
4. The people in the shelter plan their future: whole-class discussion/improvisation with teacher-in-role
5. Highly symbolic multimedia works of art are hung around the outside of the dome by the unimportant people left outside the shelter. Mobile tableaux and short YouTube-style films are performed by small groups
6. The 'important' people emerge from inside the shelter to their brave new world; a surprise is waiting for them. Whole-class improvisation with teacher as playwright-on-the-edge.

Scheme objectives

To explore a fictional post-apocalyptic world in which a decision has already been made about who should be saved and who discarded

To explore the relationships between two groups of society; can they ever reconcile their differences?

To allow the narrative to drive the participants willingness, and for them to immerse themselves in a variety of different ways of working

To develop the skill of spontaneous role-play

To offer opportunities for small group performances

To offer opportunities to evaluate their own and their peers' work.

Lesson 1: tableaux (90 mins)

Tableaux introduction

Introduce the outline to the story saying something along the lines of:

> This piece of drama is going to be set in a post-nuclear world. For the time being we are not going to worry about the actual bomb, rather we will look at a scene where people have been warned about the threat of a nuclear bomb heading for the UK. People are trying desperately to get into their town's/city's nuclear shelter to protect themselves, however, there is a problem. Only people who are deemed important by society are permitted in the shelter. The government has organised armed soldiers to protect the entrance to the shelter. Many people in this fictional story are gunned down either in cross-fire or because they posed a direct challenge to the soldiers. It is this scene that we will explore.

NUCLEAR SHELTER TABLEAUX

The whole class (using the whole space) creates a tableau depicting the moment the door of the shelter is shut with the important people safe inside. Explain that there is massive bloodshed; important people shot by accident in the confusion, unimportant people shot as they try to force their way into the shelter. Behind each of these brutal deaths lies an individual story. The aim of this session is to establish a selection of these stories.

Each participant should become aware not only of their own story but also of those around them. Everyone should establish a place in the room where they have been shot. The physicality of their death should provide an imaginative contribution to the whole class tableau. If there are blocks or steps they should consider (bearing in mind H&S) draping themselves over, around or under these for greater effect. At the point of creating their corpse they should not have a pre-planned story. This story will gradually emerge from their image and the ongoing work.

Ask each participant, one by one, to look up and see the rest of the group in the tableau and to imagine the whole scene with scenery etc. Gradually, as they wait for this to be completed, each participant should (privately and without any discussion) create their own version of events leading to this moment, inventing possible relationship ties to others in the depiction. The aim of this is to build up a variety of stories that may be used again in a later lesson.

Another tableau is then made without discussion, depicting the minute before the event above.

The class (still working as individuals) walk through the journey their character made from the first tableau to the second. As they are doing this they should begin to fill out their story in their mind.

This is repeated, with all participants simultaneously narrating their own story (out loud) as they trace the character's footsteps through the three tableaux. No-one should be listening to anyone else's narration; the whole class works simultaneously.

Action-tracking

Ask the class to action-track the moments immediately before and after (probably five seconds before and five seconds after) the central tableau. Each participant should trace the movements of their character and say out loud (with no-one listening) exactly how they are moving as factual details but not referring to the context of their movement. This is hard to do but gives an amazingly in-depth analysis of the actions, aiding understanding.

For example:

> My right foot moves forward, my left foot moves forward, my head turns. My arm reaches out and I open my hand. (This describes someone walking and then seeing someone and waving at them.)
>
> My chest caves in, my arms both move forward, my hands come in front of my chest and clutches at it as my knees buckle. My thigh hits the floor …

Students will be working in ultra slow motion so the five seconds sections can be tied in with a 40 or 60 second real-time countdown. Again, this is done as a whole group.

Sight-tracking

This is a parallel exercise to action-tracking but students are narrating solely what they see. They can include interpretations of things they actually see other participants improvising (whether or not this is the correct interpretation is irrelevant) or things that they imagine they see to make the experience more potent for themselves. Their narration must be factual and not include emotional reactions. For example:

> I see a church and a bride running away with her train streaming behind her, a man leaps out of his car. A woman with a gun shoots in the air, a man next to her shouts at her … a child cries as I walked past, she looks up at me …

Audio-tracking

The exercise will be exactly the same as the action-tracking and sight-tracking activities but on this occasion each character narrates what they hear:

> Church bells suddenly stop ringing, people are shouting, rapid gunshots are fired, the voice of a very young girl says, 'Mummy … where's my Mummy? I've lost my Mummy! Oi, Mr!'.

WHOLE CLASS RE-ENACTMENT

To finish, the whole class re-enact a 90-second sequence in real time, trying to make it as realistic as possible. They should not include any of the words from their narrations but should use the naturally-occurring speech they have decided upon. The narratives they have developed previously should inform their performances. This is re-enacted without an audience, everyone focusing on their own story. Tell them not to worry if someone does something that conflicts with what they have decided to do.

The reconstruction should last 90 seconds real time with their death at the one minute mark.

After they have died they should narrate the manner of their death in the third person.

Evaluation

The participants are asked to stand in the place where they feel they achieved their best work throughout this session and to explain what they did. They may be given the chance to comment on others' work, but be aware that this session has focused on their own contribution.

Lesson 2

SPONTANEOUS PLAYMAKING

Allocate all students to groups of between about four and five, randomly chosen.

Each group should create roles for a group who live together as a family or friends, and a web of emotionally-complicated relationships. They will need to invent back stories. They should also invent a major crisis which they are undergoing. They should not practice the scene, but should outline what they think may happen and establish a working sequence of events. They are allowed ten minutes to invent this relationship web.

Then, give two further minutes to set up the area representing the location of their scene.

All groups should play the scene simultaneously, timed to last ten minutes.

Afterwards, give students the opportunity to develop and discuss the scene and suggest any improvements they would like to make. Hand out the letter which can be developed from this outline:

> Dear ...
>
> You have been selected for a place in the city council's nuclear shelter in the event of a nuclear war. This offer is not transferable and does not extend to family members. Please inform the senior officer at the address below if you wish to take up this offer.

Explain that letters have been sent out offering specially-chosen people a place in the nuclear shelter in the event of a nuclear war.

The entrance area to the shelter should be set up at the edge of the room but in a central position of the working area. Raised blocks are set up in front of it for the soldiers to stand on.

Extra tasks

At this point, people could share some of the stories they have invented to inspire other people's improvisation work. Beware of slowing the lesson down too much though.

When walking the journey between the first two tableaux, the class can be asked to mark the place in their scene where they speak or make sounds.

Students specialising in stage design could use materials to create shelters and create a basic plan for the shelter.

If time allows, the class could repeat the scene incorporating their various improvements.

Each group decides which member has been offered a place in the shelter and why. This could mean slight changes need to be made to their back stories. They should decide (in role) if other members of their group know about the letter.

Maximum of five soldiers across the class.

Some people in some groups should elect to be secret soldiers; this in turn may affect their back stories. The soldiers should keep their prospective role a secret, although the group members will (out of role) know who who is playing the soldiers.

The group should be briefed to change scenes at this moment.

Group by group they present their scene, which is interrupted early on by a siren. There is a break in the action while one 'secret soldier' takes up position on the raised area to stop anyone gaining access without permission. The soldier will need this information before the scene begins.

At this point they should, without any planning, *spontaneously* improvise what happens in their group, as they make their way to the entrance of the shelter and encounter the individual guard.

> Will they take up their place in the shelter?
> Will anyone in the group be shot?

As different groups take their turn, encourage them to search for different outcomes to the situation. Finally the scenes are played *simultaneously*, interrupted this time by an announcement by you as teacher-in-role:

The teacher's role in this will be to observe (and if the work is to be assessed, to mark), and to act as 'playwright-on-the-edge' (PotE). In this role, the teacher can hold up the action, focus in on important moments, and allow them to be re-run if desired. PotE slows the action down and ensures that all participants are playing by the rules.

> I have to interrupt this programme. A communiqué has been received from the British Government. A warhead on an intercontinental rocket has been accidentally launched from territory 'x' 15 minutes ago. Despite efforts on from their military air force to destroy this missile it is still continuing on its journey. Unless the British and combined NATO forces are able to neutralise this missile, it will impact in the London area in 30 minutes. Please take whatever precautions you can to ensure your safety. Stay tuned to this channel for news updates.

As before in the individual scenes, the location switches to outside the shelter. This scene will be different to the one they have done in their single groups. The secret soldiers will not be dealing with a single group, so they could be distracted and will have others there to deter them from offering privileges to those they know.

Before this improvisation starts, the class could be given the opportunity to develop the design plan for the shelter, created in the previous session, by adding ground plans. What facilities would be included in a shelter in which people are going to live for the next 100 years?

This scene is exciting but needs structure. One very strict rule I always impose is that no-one is allowed to get within a certain distance of the armed guards. There will be more verbal drama if there is a distance between the different sides. The armed guards have the ultimate decision to 'shoot to kill' or 'shoot to harm' whenever they want. They do this by shouting out either one of those instructions.

Evaluation

Evaluate the work by asking the class to talk about one member of the class whose work really impressed them today.

Lesson 3

Story update

There is a massive power cut in the shelter and all communications between them and the outside world are suddenly halted. Those in the shelter take this to be the moment the explosion occurs.

However, unknown to those in the shelter, the nuclear threat has been averted and the missile did not detonate.

The unimportant people are now safe and the important people in the shelter remain completely ignorant of what has happened. These events are mirrored everywhere in the UK. The unimportant people on the surface decide to leave the important ones down below.

> **NARRATIVE/DOCUMENTARY THEATRE**
> Working on their own, or with one or two partners of their own choice, participants should devise a narrative theatre performance showing the events of the day that has since been referred to as Bloody Friday. It should be from the perspective of those who suffered a loss on the day the shelter doors were closed.

Presentation

Students should present their work and selected members of the audience should evaluate the performances they have seen.

Visual stimulus

At this point that I often show the DVD *Threads*, which gives the participants deeper knowledge of nuclear war. Many students these days are unaware of the capabilities of a nuclear bomb and are moved by the powerful TV film.

Lesson 4

Discussion

Story update

Down in the shelter the important people have begun to settle in.

After a few days a meeting is called to discuss matters that have arisen during their first few days in the shelter with the hope of making some decisions.

The narrator(s) should be (a) character(s) in the story. If a character dies in the story, they can not be a narrator unless somehow framed as a ghost. There should be a good mix of narration looking back on the event and live action dialogue.

Ideas can be developed from students' work in previous lessons. The scene should be brought to a climax by the moment of loss or the witnessing of an horrific atrocity.

Suggest that they contrast the highly-dramatic ending with a lively/comic beginning. The beginning would also benefit from being what they thought would be a significant moment in their lives e.g. a wedding, funeral, christening or perhaps an important football match like the World Cup final.

The class now represent the inhabitants of the shelter. The cast is as follows:

>> Four armed guards
>> One unimportant person who managed to get in
>> The remainder are the 'important' people.

Stress that, although this will start as a meeting, and all the points *must* be fully dealt with, movement is allowed.

This section works best if all participants use their real-life opinions so that they can effectively back up their arguments. In this section they should be themselves in this different situation.

Points for discussion

>> Is there any further use for the guns? What should happen to them?
>> How should the armed guards be viewed – as heroes or as murderers? Some who should have been occupants of the shelter were probably killed by the armed guard. Likewise, they may have killed relatives of those who did get in.
>> A can of CCTV film showing what happened just before the shelter door was shut has been discovered. What should the group in the shelter do with it? Do they want to watch it? They will, eventually, have to explain the existence of the world above the shelter but have no need to bring up the mass killings, as the whole world will (they believe) have been wiped out by the effects of the bomb. There will, in 100 years, be no trace whatsoever of what they did. Should they re-write history? What should they tell their children of the events of that day?
>> How should the groups deal with the ethical problems surrounding procreation? The group have a responsibility to create the future generation.

This is one of the lessons that often leads to discussions which continue long after the lesson has ended.

Story update

The outside world, having survived the threat of bombing, creates a new political regime. There is a fall in population due to the mass killings of Bloody Friday and the flight of political leaders to the shelters. The world becomes peaceful and, as time goes on, more prosperous and plentiful. A utopia is created as a result of the disappearance of the old political regime.

25 years on, the prosperous and happy 'unimportant' people decide they should mark the occasion of Bloody Friday with something. They decide to build a transparent, indestructible dome over the entrance to the shelter. They want to witness anyone who emerges suffocating. They wish to wreak their revenge for the lack of mercy these people showed prior to the expected nuclear explosion. They build a door to the dome with two substantial and different locks. Two families in the community are nominated key-holders. (These need to be people who genuinely believe this is an excellent thing to do).

Thinking that people's feelings towards what those in the shelter did may fade, they commission some images to hang around the dome to serve as horrific reminders of what they did on Bloody Friday.

Lesson 5

TABLEAUX YOUTUBE

In self-selected groups of between three and five, multimedia art work should be created to hang around the dome to the accompaniment of music.

The images must be abstract representations of the cruelty of the secret soldiers and the selfishness of the 'important' people on Bloody Friday.

The aim of commissioning this should be to communicate an understanding to future generations of why the doors to the dome should never be unlocked.

Once prepared, the resultant images can be performed around a circle of chairs, representing the dome.

Benjamin Britten's *War Requiem* is one musical possibility.

Each group should produce a (predominantly) non-verbal performance.

Story update

100 years later, the townsfolk in their utopian community are settling down to an enormous feast celebrating 100 years of peace and prosperity without the 'important' people. They talk about the stories of Bloody Friday that have been handed down from their ancestors.

Meanwhile a small number of people, and one babe in arms, emerge from the shelter. They are planning to begin the daunting task that they have been brought up to do - to recreate and rule a new world. To their surprise, they find themselves trapped in the transparent dome. Nearby, a group of the utopian townsfolk are tucking into a feast.

All will have been born in the shelter and will not be survivors of Bloody Friday – they are the descendants of that generation.

One of the key-holders is not there. Their key has been handed temporarily to their son/daughter.

Will the dome doors be unlocked? Will they really watch the Domers (as they have been derogatorily named) suffocate?

Lesson 6 & beyond

WHOLE-CLASS SPONTANEOUS IMPROVISATION

The emergence of the Domers

Cast four volunteers to be the four Domers emerging from the shelter into the transparent, indestructible dome. One has with a baby with them (symbolised by a white cloth or coat).

Two further volunteers take on the role of a key-holder and the second key-holder's offspring. The key-holder initiates the improvisation with a pre-prepared speech celebrating the last 100 years.

During the meal the four emerge. What will happen? The session will work best if participants work from their own opinions; they shouldn't say something just to make the story better. There is no specific intended outcome. Whatever is decided can be built upon.

Give the roles of the key-holders to whoever has spoken out most vociferously against the important people.

The teacher takes on a PotE role and also imposes times when each of the Domers should die.

Possible developments

>> If all the Domers end up dying, someone from a neighbouring town could arrive who was released from their dome but expelled from the city?

>> If the baby is released, but none of the other Domers, how will it be brought up?

>> If some of the Domers are released what would be a good follow-up story for one of them? What positive or negative predicaments could they be put in?

Evaluation

Tell students to stand in the place where they achieved their best work in the latest whole-group piece of work and write down what they did and why it was successful. This can be repeated to show other participants' best overall contribution.

Missing Dan Nolan

Missing Dan Nolan,
Mark Wheeller
(2004, dbda)
ISBN: 978-1-902843-16-2

Introduction

Before Edexcel introduced the new specification unit 2 (interpreting a complete and substantial play text) to their GCSE exam, I admit I had never previously taught any complete plays per se as part of my CSE/GCSE courses. Occasionally groups selected to present a play for the performance paper but that was the exception in our school, rather than the rule. I felt this new idea was good for the course and I liked the way that the original specification supported teachers by suggesting how it could be structured.

Initially I decided I would take an Arthur Miller play, *All My Sons*, which would – I thought – be appealing to boys; at my school we have boy-heavy groups. I developed a scheme of work for this and it went well, but it stuck out like a sore thumb from the rest of the course. It was the only part of the course where students were asked to explore a totally naturalistic text, something I encouraged them to avoid when developing devised work. I wanted a play that modelled physical theatre techniques to assist them with their work in the performance paper.

I decide to start using my own plays, initially using *Hard to Swallow* purely because I had heard other schools were using it. I then moved on to use *Legal Weapon* and most recently *Missing Dan Nolan*. This has a male-dominated cast, where girls can also enjoy playing boys, and challenging opportunities for girls in the roles of Pauline (Dan's mother) and Sarah (Dan's school friend). The other factor in my decision is that the central characters are all the same age as students studying for a GCSE so they find it easy to relate to the characters and situations. It seemed a perfect match and has, without doubt, proved to be the case.

Background to the play

I had originally seen posters announcing Dan Nolan's disappearance early in January 2002 while walking my dogs in Southampton. As there had been nothing on the television about Dan, I assumed that he had been found or perhaps that he was not missing after all. When I realised that he was still missing I explained the lack of media coverage to myself by thinking his disappearance must somehow be less important, serious or was likely to be resolved quickly.

Then one day in April 2002 I saw a stall outside my local supermarket with a 'Dan Nolan missing' banner above it. I couldn't imagine how such a stall could help, so approached and discovered that they were trying to raise awareness. They had found it very difficult to get media coverage. As a parent myself I was shocked. How would I feel if my son or daughter went missing and I was not able to convey this fact to the public through the media?

To cut a long story short, I offered to write a dramatic reconstruction (also raising any other issues Dan's story might throw up) to help raise awareness about Dan's disappearance. I approached four Oakland's Youth Theatre members to become committed to the project. It was crucial to get the show on the road to help Dan's parents in their quest for more media coverage sooner rather than later.

As I came within a mile of the Nolan's family home in the village of Hamble, Southampton, for my first interview, I saw posters plastered to every one of the 30 or 40 trees and lampposts in the vicinity. It conveyed all too clearly the impression of a very loving family on a determined, if not desperate, search for a much-loved son.

One of the first things I saw as I went into the Nolan's house to do my first interview was the photo I'd seen of Dan in the missing posters in its original school-photo-style frame. The photo, in its original setting was so poignant. I remembered my own school photos that I had always wanted to hide and wondered what Dan had thought of this one, not knowing that it was destined to become so well-known for such a dreadful moment in his life.

I decided that the documentary style of writing I had seen Roy Nevitt use at Stantonbury and had used successfully myself for two earlier plays (*Graham* and *Too Much Punch for Judy*) was the best way to approach this play.

It was crucial to convey the facts and opinions in the way that the people who had experienced this situation first-hand had phrased them. Consequently, *Missing Dan Nolan* uses the words of Dan's family, friends (who were with him the night he disappeared) and the detective in charge of the investigation, to try to get as close to the truth of events as their memories will allow.

On interviewing the friends who shared that fateful evening with Dan, I was struck by their youth. They were, as I imagine Dan was, normal 14/15 year-old boys.

Tragically, in 2003, his family's (and the wider community's) hopes of Dan returning home were dashed when remains found on a remote beach in Swanage were identified as Dan's. However, Dan's family and friends remain supportive of what the play can continue to do:

> 'Although we've lost our Dan, I feel very proud. All the issues about Dan's disappearance and the safety issues surrounding teenagers are in the play and it must continue to raise awareness.'
>
> Pauline Nolan (Dan's mother)

Performance advice

I would like to take this opportunity to say something about the style of performance needed for a documentary or reality play such as this. These words will help any students exploring the play text.

It must at all times be remembered when reading or performing this play that the events it portrays are as close to the truth as memory and honesty allows. The performers should not

---

Documentary plays use the words of those interviewed (in this case – Pauline, Greg, Clare, Thom, Joe, Sarah, Andy and Detective Superintendent Stewart) unaltered; where there is dialogue it is fleshed out but still based closely on what was said in the original interviews with the author. The author may have altered the tense of a sentence and there may be occasional linking words added but the idea is to get as close to the truth as memory will permit.

impersonate the real-life characters (it is unlikely that they will know them to be able to do so) but breathe into them a life that is a reasonable interpretation of the words in the script. Unless specifically instructed to do otherwise for a particular effect, the actors should avoid overstatement and veer towards underplaying. Trust the material. It is after all as near to possible a realistic account of events.

Missing Dan Nolan

The scheme

Lesson 1

Read-through

One problem this unit poses is how to get your class to know the script without boring them with read-throughs that take for ever. Andy Kempe introduced me to a magnificent way of introducing texts to students:

Divide the class into five groups and the play into five sections:

>> Group 1 – sections 1 and 2
>> Group 2 – sections 3 and 4
>> Group 3 – section 5
>> Group 4 – section 6 up to and including Jo's line that starts: 'My last image of Dan …' on page 43 of the current edition of the play
>> Group 5 – section 6 from 'My last image of Dan …' on page 43 of the current edition of the play.

The groups don't cast the read through. They read the text around their group. So person one takes line one, person two, line two and so on. If they come across a speech which is inordinately long, (which they will in this play) it should be divided up sentence by sentence.

All words should be read, including (importantly) the stage instructions.

There are many advantages to this way of reading a script:

>> No time is wasted in casting
>> Weaker readers are protected from over-exposure
>> No one has nothing to do; conversely no one has too much to do, which they may enjoy but everyone else gets bored with
>> Because each group member is only ever a maximum of four lines from their turn, they will keep following the script
>> There is no need for people to skip through the script to figure out what they have to read, given their allocated part, thus concentration is improved.

Once the groups have completed the reading they can start working on their first task.

STILL IMAGE

Each group creates still images to show key moments from the section they have been reading. They are allowed to use captions but they must be lines from the play.

It is a good idea to discuss the elements that make a good still image and I would expect the following to come out of this discussion:

>> Use of levels

>> Use of meaningful spatial relationships

>> Opportunities for actors to be physically off-balance to ensure maximum tension/strength in bodies

>> Opportunities for symbolism

>> Facial expressions that convey clear feelings.

When all the groups have finished preparing their images they show them in chronological order. The teacher can fill in any narrative gaps so that the others watching the images begin to get a picture of where the section they have been reading fits into the whole play.

Remaining in their previous groupings, students should now select key lines from the section they have read that typify each of the characters. Each individual in each group learns one of these lines and prepares to deliver them to others as though they are that character.

For example, if I were in group 1, I might choose:

Pauline: I wake up every day thinking we could get some vital information. However I realise it's probably just another day I've got to face.

Or more simply and succinctly:

Dan: Can I go fishing?

As with the lines above, it is important that it is obvious who said them.

LINE EXCHANGE

Once each person in the group has selected their line, everyone in the class is asked to mill around the room presenting their lines to each other (in character) in random ever-changing pairs. While doing this they should try to make a mental note of anyone who they think is saying a line originating from the same character they are playing. Then (without any talking other than using their line) they should group themselves according to the character they are playing; so, for example, all the Dans should group together.

Once grouped (in silence), the lines are presented publicly and each person has an opportunity to regroup themselves should they decide they have ended up in the wrong group. It is best to do this exercise, delaying as much as possible an overt revelation as to who everyone is playing. It is possible now that some people are in very small groups if they have selected a character who only plays a small part in the play. You may choose to group these people with other related characters in the play in readiness for the next exercise.

Once in these new character groups, using all the lines (selected by the group of Dans, for example) as captions, they should present a new still image that somehow represents this character in the play. It can be an image that shows the character's journey or a more symbolic image.

Once completed, each group should evaluate their own work and highlight aspects that they would like to draw the teacher/assessor's attention towards. After this, others (not in the performing group) should offer positive evaluation which might usefully arise from the self-evaluation comments.

Lesson 2

Getting under the skin of the characters

When I teach this lesson, I arrange the class in a loose triangle/semi-circle and sit at the apex of this shape. I then get them to interview me as the playwright (my colleague does this exercise as though he is the director). I allow them a short while to prepare some intelligent questions which will provide them with further insight into the play. You are thus modelling the way in which hot-seating is done while also taking the opportunity to convey a lot of information.

HOT-SEATING

Seven volunteers adopt the roles of Pauline, Greg, Sarah, Thom, Joe, Andy and the night watchman Gaffa (who fascinates my students).

I seat them in different corners of our drama studio in the following groups:

1. Pauline, Greg and Sarah
2. Thom and Joe
3. Andy (he could equally be placed with Thom and Joe)
4. Night Watchman

As before, I give the reporters (remainder of the class) *short* preparation time during which they can talk to other reporters to decide what questions they should ask.

I stress that in their role as reporters (much as mine was, as the playwright) they can ask important, searching questions, which in everyday conversation may be deemed inappropriate. They should, however, be sensitive.

The reporters can work alone or in pairs.

Each reporter chooses who they wish to interview first and heads towards their target interviewee. They can stay with them for as long or as short a length of time as they wish.

There may be some periods of the lesson where some characters are not being interviewed.

I allow the interviews to continue for about 20 minutes, which gives the reporters enough time to amass information and me enough time to get round to assess everyone if required.

Once finished, we discuss how each of the roles felt during the interview, or rather how they think they would have felt if they were the real person. I also ask them which questions stuck in their mind; this can highlight good work by the reporters that may have gone unnoticed. Finally, the reporters have their say; what did they think of the answers they were given?

This rarely happens in practice but is possible, particularly in smaller classes.

Forum theatre one

This scene is based on the night I visited the families of Joe and Thom (Dan's friends who were with him on the fishing trip the night he disappeared) by prior arrangement. The facts I tell my students are as follows and can be told by other teachers by reading this passage if wanted, or saying it as though they have heard me talking/writing about it:

> 'By this point I felt totally committed to the cause of writing this play with a view to supporting the uncovering of information that might help reveal Dan's whereabouts and to promote the case to a criminal investigation rather than a missing person case. I had also told Dan's family that the play was being planned.
>
> 'Unbeknown to me, Joe and Thom felt blamed for Dan's disappearance, partly as a result of a website which had been hurriedly set up; they felt it suggested that both of them had left Dan on his own that night and failed to explain any of the reasons why this happened.
>
> 'Joe's and Thom's parents were all there and, as I remember, Joe and Thom arrived later on.
>
> 'It was a sunny evening. The meeting was held in Thom's family's garden.
>
> 'As a result of the meeting, both Joe and Thom agreed to be interviewed and it was decided by them that Andy (Thom's father) should represent the families of the two boys in the play as a spokesperson."

It did become a criminal investigation and the play was very much a part of the campaign that made this happen.

For the purposes of this exercise it is not important to say how the meeting actually went (beyond the facts above) but it is interesting for students to meet in groups and decide what their attitude, as the two families, might be. Consequently, the meeting can be run a number of times (forum-style) to see how the Mark Wheeller role deals with the different situations he encounters.

Forum theatre two

When I was researching the play, I remember seeing something – or rather, not seeing something, which made a deep impression on me and led to this second forum theatre exercise being developed.

As I described in the introduction to this scheme, when I drove for the first time into Hamble, where Dan and his friends lived, there were posters everywhere – on trees, bus stops, in shops and house windows. However, when I went to interview Thom and Joe, I couldn't help noticing that they had no posters on display in their house at all. It made me wonder how their family had come to that decision and it is this imagined discussion about this that makes for the central area of exploration in this forum theatre exercise.

Volunteers are selected for the role-play, each having decided privately their own way of dealing with this emotive situation. There should be no discussion, as there would have been no discussion in the real situation:

In this brief encounter,
how much does Thom/
Joe give away about
what he is feeling
about the request?
This moment provides
a great opportunity for
subtlety in the portrayal
of Thom/Joe.

>> Clare Nolan, Dan's sister, calls round to Thom's (or Joe's) house
>> This is the first time that she has seen Thom/Joe since Dan's disappearance
>> Clare hands a poster to Thom/Joe, who takes it
>> Clare requests that his family put it up on their property to raise awareness.
>> Clare leaves the scene and Thom/Joe and his parents meet
>> They decide not to put the poster up on their property.

I have been fascinated by the results of this role-play and the amazing empathy the students have to all parties in this complex situation. It allows them to make more thoughtful interpretations of what we know of the characters, and helped me to understand something I struggled with for a while after I'd conducted the interviews.

At the end of this session, in silence, students write an in-role diary entry for one of the characters from this session. The diary entry can be from a date of their choice. I normally suggest the following dates to give them a starting point but this list is by no means exhaustive:

>> The night following the day Dan went missing
>> The night it is learnt that a play is to be written about Dan's disappearance
>> The night of Mark Wheeller's visit
>> The first night of the play
>> 1st January at midnight; exactly a year after Dan's disappearance.

Lesson 3: marking the moment

I use this session to explore the separation of the boys.

The technique of **marking the moment** is defined by Edexcel in their excellent 2000 specification as:

> Freezing action; using captions from the text rearranged; inner thoughts spoken out loud; using lighting to spotlight a moment etc ... revealing significance for the individual in terms of revealing an inner understanding, an insight or evoking a feeling about the issue or idea being explored.

It is a great technique to use regardless of whether or not you are teaching Edexcel GCSE.

I recommend groups use end of Section 6 (page 43 in the edition I have) where Thom is faced with the impossible dilemma of whether he should follow his drunken mate (Joe) home or go and help Dan with his fishing equipment, which he had needed help with on the way to the pontoon. This section allows significant lines to resonate in the boys' heads, the obvious one being:

Pauline: 'Now remember … there are weirdos about so keep your noses clean and stick together.'

There are of course others. It encourages students to consider placement of characters and relationships. Dan seems like the central character but in this scene it should be Thom. All students will empathise with this situation and this will motivate them to produce more adventurous work. I try to ensure that students are not just presenting a glorified freeze-frame by getting them to think in a filmic way.

I generally give them a handout with the following information on it:

> In this section you should aim to make good use of the following:
> >> Climax/anticlimax
> >> Rhythm and pace
> >> Contrasts
> >> Characterisation
> >> Use of symbol.

After the presentations, there should be evaluations. This time I ask the audience to proffer evaluative comments first before the group have a chance to highlight what they would like the audience to take note of.

Lesson 4

Some of the students I teach have difficulty reading so I chose to focus on the opening moments of the play here, where much if it is movement-based. This section basically recaps the reconstructed short version of what happened to the boys on the pontoon, set to an atmospheric musical soundtrack.

Encourage students to select appropriate elements of drama (listed in lesson 3) to present this extract.

After you have given instructions detailing the important elements they should consider for performance, the students will group themselves to stage the opening page of the play. I play the suggested soundtrack (as loud as possible) and talk over it saying where the action fits with the music, so I am clearly structuring the work but leaving how they will actually manifest these ideas up to them.

If you have the opportunity, this would be a good time to allow the students to stage Section 6 of the play. There is scope for naturalistic acting in the first section and also the opportunity to explore ways of clarifying the encounter between Thom and Greg (who isn't naturally in the scene) for the audience.

Students with technical expertise could set up a simple lighting state for this scene which lends itself well to creative lighting. I would suggest blue cover signifying the time of night and a strong moonlight signified by floor lights shining up onto the boys' faces, which will also cast grotesque shadows on the back wall. Note this is but one option. Clever questioning by the teacher should lead the student to develop their own response to the possibilities for the lighting for this scene.

This section of the play is reproduced below:

Section 1: noodles and out!

Silent Night by Sinead O'Connor plays. Thom, Joe, George and Dan enter and set up for some fishing. All are wearing clothes suitable for a cold night's fishing but enter in a lively manner counterpointing the sombre music. Dan wears a grey Henri Lloyd jacket, blue cotton trousers and Airforce blue DCs with the laces untied. The boys are lit as though by moonlight. They drink from a vodka bottle and as they do so the mood changes. Music with a skate-punk ('All the Small Things' by Blink 182) feel fades in underneath the Sinead O'Connor song. Thom and Jo begin to mess around involving Dan and George in their japes. Amongst other things, they prank call to George's mobile and laugh. George leaves. Joe and Thom continue to lark around energetically. Finally Joe is sick. Thom is in a dilemma as to who he should leave with (Joe or Dan) but finally decides to help Joe home. Dan remains on his own. The lights crossfade to establish a lighting state suggesting Dan's home. Dan begins to 'headbang'. Clare enters angrily.

Clare: *(Shouting over the music.)* Turn it down, Dan!

Dan: *(Shouting over the music.)* What?

Clare: *(Shouting over the music.)* Turn it down!

Dan: *(The music stops.)* That better is it?

Clare: You're so selfish playing all that banging stuff so loud!

Dan: Well I'm out tonight so you can play Westlife up full and prance around as much as you like!

Clare: We're a typical brother/sister … 18 months apart. *(Laughing.)* We compete to see who can play the loudest music.

Dan: *(Dan is getting his stuff together to go out.)* No contest!

Clare: He's got a better CD player than me so he always wins.

Missing Dan Nolan, Mark Wheeller (2004, dbda).

Lesson 5: individual monologue

I kick this session off with a brief introduction to delivering published monologues.

>> What are the points to consider when performing a monologue?
>> How can you pace the speech and animate what, on the page, appears to be still?

I normally select one reasonably short monologue to read chorally (as a whole class) with the punctuation being read as full words i.e. by saying 'full stop' where they appear. This allows students to become aware of the pace and the importance of punctuation.

Each student then selects their own monologue and, being fully aware of pace, rhythm, intonation and action in their presentation they learn and rehearse the speech for homework.

I came across this exercise in a Royal Shakespeare Company workshop.

Students should have an opportunity to evaluate the work they present. I generally get them to do self-evaluation by asking the to walk through their monologue on stage explaining each decision they made with reference to every move or change in vocal delivery. This walking-through serves to remind them of what they did and normally assists the detail of the evaluation enormously.

Further opportunities can be offered to the students by getting them to adapt a set of newspaper articles telling the same topical story from different perspectives or different slants. The exploration of this text should give the students an idea of how documentary plays work. I suggest you are not too ambitious with the original material – too much initial material could well put them off forever!

Cultures

Introduction

I have realised, by looking through these schemes of work, how creative I was in my early teaching career in terms of developing imaginative lessons. Most of these schemes came from the early period of my career. I think perhaps I've come to a point where I present my most successful lessons because I want young people to have fun with them as I have seen other others do in the past. I remember enjoying the days though where no two classes would ever have the same lesson. It was high-pressured, high-risk and very time-consuming in terms of planning. As David Bowie says in one of his song lyrics, 'when it's good it's really good and when it's bad I fall to pieces'. The same was true of my lessons; when they succeeded they were amazingly rewarding, but when they didn't, they were unmitigated failures the like of which I tend not to have nowadays!

At Stantonbury I remember 'drama specials' being organised on a number of occasions, . These took drama out of the normal constraints of the timetable and showed other departments what our subject was all about. It was tremendous publicity for drama and meant that the department became highly respected by other curriculum areas. Some of these special sessions would involve up to six classes working simultaneously in spontaneous role-play exercises. Normally the climax of these days would be a huge and exciting (in-role) meeting of all the participating students and teachers.

My move to St John's School in Epping offered me the opportunity to translate the ideas I had accumulated at Stantonbury to a school where the drama department was pretty much non-existent and I was the only drama teacher. One idea I was keen to implement was that of the drama special. This kind of work is so good at showing other teachers (and students) the power of drama methodology and is an exciting departure from the everyday curriculum where subjects are taught as discrete, compartmentalised units. I have heard drama teachers saying that our subject should not be used across curriculum as it becomes a service subject – this is, in my experience, nonsense! It works to educate other teachers about the power of drama and elicits respect for the subject the like of which I have not seen in schools where drama remains isolated in its own area of the school.

This cultures scheme of work was developed for a humanities project in my time at Epping. I remember it being so successful that I was asked to repeat it each year and went on to use it a number of times in Southampton as well.

If you have two groups of 30 it may be worth considering splitting them into three groups of 20 and asking for an additional teacher.

This 'cultures' scheme is designed for three full-size classes of anything up to 30 students with three teacher/facilitators in three different teaching spaces set up for drama. One of the spaces will need to be particularly big as all the classes will end up here. I would suggest that the optimum class size is 20. In a typical five-hour school day the following structure would be ideal. I have only presented this session with KS3 groups but that does not mean it can only work with students of this age.

The scheme

Scheme structure

Lesson 1 (2.5 hours)

This session is used to establish the three different communities. There will be time for planning and then rehearsing the created culture.

Lesson 2 (1 hour)

This session will be an exchange programme where two students from each community will visit one of the other communities to get a feel for how they live.

Lesson 3 (1 hour)

A disaster befalls two of the communities and they both evacuate their land to seek refuge with the third community.

Lesson 4 (30 mins)

This is an important opportunity for all students to reflect on what they have done throughout the day, as well as evaluate what they have learnt. It can either be done in their original groups, in random mixed groups and/or as a written exercise.

Lesson 1: establishing the communities

Each class meets with their teacher/facilitator in a separate classroom/drama space.

To provide a fictional context for the work, my colleague Bernard Andrews contributed the following scene-setting paragraph:

Resources:

Large paper/cloth for flag

A3 (minimum) sheets of paper for the dictionary

A selection of natural props (twigs, stones etc) – these may be useful to inspire at various points in the morning session.

Just before the apocalypse of planet Earth, small groups of humans were evacuated in spacecrafts. Only a few of these groups survived, but they managed to eek out an existence on remote planets that had vaguely hospitable atmospheres. Some 500,000 years later, evolution has taken its effect on these communities and their individual oral traditions have become far removed from their original basis.

In this session we will focus on three islands on one of these planets who become aware of each others' existence.

Each group is required to name the island that they are living on.

In each group (island) the teacher/facilitator divides the students into five equal groups. Each sub-group is given one of the tasks outlined below. They will have up to 45 minutes to complete their task and plan the way in which they will present their conclusions to the rest of the class. Everyone in each group should have something to do in preparation for the rehearsed presentation, which will be shown at the end of this lesson. The presentation should take the form of a peer-led lesson which will involve the whole-class participation in the activities which have been invented. I suggest that task sheets are prepared for each group.

For now I will call them Island 1, Island 2 and Island 3. The students will be far more imaginative than I am in their suggestions.

TASK 1 – CEREMONY

Develop a ceremony which reveals which figure your community worships and what rituals you use to perform this worship. The group should also create stories, which would have been handed down from generation to generation in their society; these will explain more about the history and belief system of their island. For part of the ceremony, students will need to tell (or, even better, act out) some of their stories. The ceremony will be taught by this task group to the whole island group and must offer opportunities for all to be actively involved.

TASK 2 – DICTIONARY

Develop a simple dictionary, listing the keywords your culture uses when communicating with each other. The dictionary should only include pictorial definitions as there should be no recognisable English words in this community. This group will also create greetings (ways in which they greet each other in the morning or after not seeing each other for a long time).

This group's presentation will demonstrate the greeting(s) and ask the class to imitate them in randomly-paired meetings set up by the teacher. The group working on the greeting demonstration task should then lead a rote learning-style lesson using the keywords from the dictionary.

At this stage the group will be teaching in their own language. It would be a really effective development if short improvised situations, rather like those you'd find in a foreign language phrase book, could be set up to get the class using the language.

TASK 3 – LEADERSHIP AND MEDICINE

In order to determine how decisions are made and how people are organised politically, someone in the group will become the leader. Does this person have any actual power and if so, how much? If not, what is expected of them? The leader will be chosen by the whole island group during this task group's presentation.

This task group is also to create beliefs in various remedies using plants readily available in the environment where they live. One person from this task group is granted special powers of healing. This person must orchestrate a healing ceremony that requires the whole group to be present and can only occur on a particular calendar date; this means the healer doesn't have unlimited powers of healing, but they do have exceptional value to the community. How will this person be treated in light of their supernatural gifts? Will they have different living quarters, guards etc.?

In their presentation, this task group will need to explain how this community organises itself, then the decision as to who will be their leader can be made. This person should (unlike the healer) be selected from the whole island group.

The role (and identity) of the healer will need to be explained.
They will teach the other task groups the whole-group role-play of a healing ceremony which will be rehearsed.

TASK 4 – FURTHERING THE RACE

This group must create the way in which their culture procreates. This must be an imaginative and entirely asexual activity. It will bear no relation to how procreation occurs in the human race and need not be scientifically possible. It may be necessary for the group to propose laws about the number of offspring each family are allowed to have. This task group's presentation will outline the rules they have developed to the rest of the group and lead the whole island group in a role-play of their method of procreation.

An example might be: 'The hairs of two people are taken and put in piece of cloth and placed in the linden tree. One year later, a baby will appear in the cloth under the tree. Whoever picks the baby up, delivers it to the two hair-givers. They will be responsible for the upbringing of the baby.

TASK 5 – RE-ENERGISING

How does this community re-energise? As with the procreation task this need not be scientifically possible and need not be like the sleep of humans. One example could be to create 're-energy time' where everyone goes to the place of the linden tree and picks up a small twig and holds it in their ear, standing on one leg. This is their sleep position. The feeding should not be oral and should be an activity that is always conducted as a whole group.

Once the groups have completed their tasks (each lasting about 30 minutes) bring them all together and each group should deliver their presentation as described above, so that the rest of the island group can learn about the cultural traditions that they are to adopt.

Flags and anthems

Each separate task group should produce either a flag, which communicates something of the history of their community, or a song (or rap) exclusively in their new language which is to become their national anthem.

Once completed, the flag and the anthem are selected by a vote, cast by all community members. The anthem will be learnt by the whole community.

Stress how important it is for the community to have this as part of their identity.

Community roles

The final activity of this session is for the class to decide on each student's role within the community. Each person should be assigned a different role. This will need to be illustrated by some special activity or responsibility that can be undertaken as part of the following exercise.

Once this is established they should work out an order of events to occur over the period of one whole day. Most events will be communal but there will be some time where individuals go about their own business according to their role.

Finally, the whole class should go on to role-play a speed run of a day in the life of their community. This needs to include opportunities for each of the completed tasks to be displayed and for each person to show their individual contribution to the community and to be rehearsed.

At this point, when I have run this session previously, there is normally a natural (school) break. I stress to all the participants that the sessions will work best if they do not talk about what they have been doing to students in the different island groups.

Lesson 2: the exchange

I recommend that after the break, groups remain in their home classrooms (islands) to have a complete run through of the day-in-the life role play.

At a predetermined time arranged with the other teachers (from the other two islands) each teacher should announce to their island that there is to be an exchange programme between the three islands.

Each group selects two people, who will each travel alone to the other islands to experience a day in the life of the different island. The two travellers need to be confident students as this is a situation where they could feel overexposed.

> The travellers should be chosen with care; it would probably not be advisable to allow the leader or healer to go on this journey as they are too important to the home community.

From island 1: one person will go to island 2 and another person will travel to island 3

From island 2: one person will go to island 1 and another to island 3

From island 3: one person will go to island 1 and another to island 2.

Each group decides upon an appropriate gift that they can take to the island which is hosting them.

The traveller is only allowed to speak in the language of their home island i.e. no English. They should aim to pick up some of the language of the island they are visiting and are (obviously) permitted to speak to their hosts in their own language. Likewise, the islanders who are receiving the exchange person can use any language they pick up from their exchange person. Privately, the host island can use English when speaking outside the earshot of the visitors.

The travellers should take anything they need with them in order to survive. In the example I gave about re-energising, both members of that community would have needed to take a twig with them to the separate islands they are visiting and look after it, otherwise they will starve.

There will be a short pause for discussions as the travellers move from island to island. In each group you should ensure that everyone is aware of what they are to do when the travellers from the other two islands arrive. They are to show their visitors a typical day in their community's life. You should initiate a discussion with the islanders as to whether they want their prospective visitors to watch the day in the life or if they should try to encourage them to become a part of it. How will they deal with the visitor if they do not want to do what is expected of them (i.e they may want the visitor to watch but the visitor may want to join in)?

Playwright-on-the-edge

During the exchange, take on the role of playwright on the edge (PotE) by directing, facilitating and perhaps manipulating the ongoing improvisation. You will have the power to freeze the action and act as a voiceover to issue instructions to the islanders.

When the travellers arrive on the different islands the group should greet their visitors. They may well need to be reminded by the teacher (PotE) that their island greetings are all different. Consequently they will have to teach their visitors their greeting (using only gesture and the language of their island) before anything else can happen. Each person in the group should greet each of the two visitors to welcome them onto their island. The two visitors will need to greet each of the island inhabitants to see that they have all learnt how to perform the required exchange. The visitors will need to hand over their gift and try, through gesture and their own language, to explain what the gift is and what it means to their people.

Once the greetings are completed, guide the islanders to demonstrate their day in the life. The visitors may at times be invited to participate in the events or, alternatively, be placed in a position where they are a spectator.

There will come a time when the visitor is offered food. If each island's way of re-energising is radically different then this will be impossible to teach to outsiders. The visitor should therefore find an appropriate place to undergo their own energy-giving activity alone.

When the day in the life is completed the visitors should be given an opportunity to thank their hosts and then leave the island they have been visiting and return to their home island.

Once they have left, the islanders should (in English) offer opinions about their visitors and how they feel their island was perceived by the outsiders.

The travellers will then return to their home island and share their experiences on the two islands they visited with their own community. The community will also share with the travellers what has happened on their own soil. This sharing time is likely to be cut short by the natural end of the session; again, reiterate that it is best they don't speak about the ongoing drama to other students participating in the day.

At no point should any English language words be used in public speech.

As PotE, you should avoid becoming a translator as this will remove the learning involved in islanders learning how to communicate with each other. Confusion and misunderstandings aren't necessarily negative.

In my experience all of the groups will have a lot to talk about at this point.

Lesson 3: the natural disaster

Make the following announcement:

> A natural disaster has befallen islands 2 and 3 and they have no choice but to evacuate. They will become refugees on island 1 as there is nowhere else for them to go. How will the community of island 1 cope with the fact that their neighbours now need to live with them on their island?
>
> People from island 2 and 3 have now been rescued from their respective islands and are embarking on a journey to island 1. No one knows how they will be received. No one knows how they will feel. Suddenly, island 1 will have twice as many refugees on their island as they have indigenous people.
>
> How will the three islands cope together?
>
> How will they communicate?
>
> Can the travellers from the exchange programme help to instigate communication between the three islands who do not speak the same languages or share the same customs?

Make it clear to all the island groups that they can speak in modern English when they are alone in their own group but when they speak to other islanders they must only communicate in the language of their own island and any words they have picked up from the other islanders. The exchanges become of central importance to this session as they have some knowledge of at least one other island community.

At this point, all islanders from island 2 and 3 should be taken (in an orderly fashion) to island 1. There they will encounter the indigenous people of that island.

Meanwhile, on island 1, the islanders will discuss what kind of welcome they are going to give to their new community members and talk about other implications of this crisis.

The lead teacher should take on the role of PotE and move this final session gently through the developing narrative, which can vary dramatically according to the imagination of your students. The teacher as PotE has to be ready to follow the story and to provoke discussion by asking students leading questions.

For the final half an hour, the students should return to their original island groups, or be mixed into new groups, and evaluate the work they have undertaken during the day.

Horror House

Background

In October 2008 I ran a workshop at the NATD conference based on the teaching of my plays, which was well received. More importantly though, my lasting impression of the conference was participating in Luke Abbott's Mantle of the Expert workshop (Luke was my former head of department at Stantonbury).

There were a number of weird things about this workshop: firstly it came at a time when I had just been appointed to undertake cross-curricular drama work in other departments at the newly-formed Oasis Academy Lord's Hill; secondly, when Luke returned to Stantonbury after doing his MA with Dorothy Heathcote, I left to go to Epping so was never able to benefit from what he had learnt in that year. Finally, I had had brief encounters with what I understood to be Mantle of the Expert (MotE) but had enjoyed none of them, feeling they were static and a bit boring. My mistake was seeing them through the eyes of a drama teacher. MotE, I discovered, was a great way of teaching other curriculum areas using drama to stimulate interest in a range of topics. It is the best method that I have found which effectively uses drama methodology in a traditional classroom set-up. This couple of hours opened up a new way of working for me and one that, late-on in my career, is opening up opportunities to create brand new schemes of work.

I returned to the my school and planned a single lesson (dipping my toe in the water) for our Year 7s to introduce myself to them and to kick-off my new role of using drama across the school's curriculum. The lesson may well not have been 'proper' MotE but whatever it was it worked fantastically well. I hope it will offer teachers a starting point with which to experiment or perhaps develop further – I certainly plan to do so.

The lesson

At the time, I was working with a Year 8 student at risk of exclusion, Jodie, who has a real enthusiasm for drama. The Year 7s had, in some cases, no previous experience of drama – some even displayed a prejudice about participating. None of the groups knew me but most knew Jodie, which proved invaluable. The lesson lasted for approximately an hour and was to lead into creative writing work. I wanted to develop a structure that would guarantee me – a stranger – their full attention.

I remembered Cecily O'Neill's 'Haunted House' work and thought an idea like this would appeal to both sexes in Year 7. Having Jodie as my 'actor in residence' was a gift; I decided that she would represent a ghost, Alice.

When Dorothy Heathcote saw the manuscript for this book she was concerned that, by including this, I may serve to perpetuate the myth that 'MotE is, or can be, a short-term enterprise lesson, the latest trick in the teacher's pack of possibilities.' I have included this brief experiment merely to show my ongoing learning as a teacher testing out a new way of working that excited me. I started small. Since doing this I have undertaken more developed MotE work. I do not want this session to contribute to any such myths and hope that it will be viewed in the context in which I have written it in – 'trying out an idea'.

A 'company' (responsible team) was set up to buy properties for use as horror house-style entertainment venues. These houses were not situated in theme parks, but on normal streets. In my introduction to the company (in-role) I told them how successful they had already become, having captured the public's interest and made much out of cheap, run-down properties. I said their success had led to all of them receiving a bonus of £1000. The class then duly felt confident in their ability from the start of the lesson!

As with any dramatic situation, I needed a problem for the class to solve – a problem I had no answer to. I showed a photograph of a modern property that had not been looked after and said that, although it was not the sort of property we would normally buy, the owner was saying that this was genuinely haunted. Should we buy it? I suggested an extortionate price tag, even though it had no electricity and was inhospitable. I explained that I had been dubious, but the owner had invited me over to see for myself.

At this point, I faded in music: Steve Harley's *Innocence and Guilt* (available on iTunes – it works best if you can loop the introduction). This set up a disturbing, childlike atmosphere. The music underscored my speech and Jodie – or Alice as we called her, who up until this point had been drawing – became our focus, acting out what I said as I relived the moment:

> There was a room upstairs the owner had locked. He wouldn't let me see inside unless I returned at midnight.
> When I did, I saw a girl drinking a glass of wine. I could see right through the girl and even put my hand through her. Suddenly she looked around, as though she'd been distracted. She dropped the glass ... but instead of it shattering on the floor, it disintegrated. I turned and noticed the man who was selling the house had gone. Finally, Alice disintegrated and when I looked on her table there were the drawings she'd been doing. The man (who had returned) interrupted me from looking and said, 'if you want to see those you must buy the house'.
>
> (music fades)
>
> So do we want to buy this place, or at least investigate its potential further? I have an invitation to take you there if you'd like to go.

A discussion ensued. Each class I taught was keen to visit the house and assess it. I moved the one or two individual students who didn't want to join us and sat them next to Jodie to 'watch'. I had to hatch a plan pretty quickly to involve them – and I did!

Everyone else, in a very brief mime (demonstrated by myself with the previous musical underscore), found one object from the house that would contribute to the story. They literally stood up, bent down and picked up the object (mimed) using the music as the cueing device. Each person, in turn, ritualistically placed their (mimed) object on the table in front of Alice (and the non participants) and told them (but not the class, creating a mystery) what the object was. When all the 'objects' are on the table, Alice selected the one she most treasures and placed it safely somewhere in the room. Where, out of role, the whole class can see.

My idea for the non-participant(s) was that they should undergo a memory test of the objects placed on the table. How many can they remember? As the list is recalled, I commented on how they may be used in the story and/or got suggestions from the students. The problem here is working out how to use objects thrown in to challenge the teacher. Often these were up-to-date objects, or drops of blood. This led me to ask the question: 'Is this a set-up by the seller of the house? If so how is Alice created? It may, for us as the company, be advantageous for Alice not to be a real ghost. If she's an elaborate trick (such as a hologram) then we can replicate her in all of our existing houses as well!'

Finally, we used forum theatre to create a scene where, among other ideas, some of the company attempt to take the object Alice has hidden to see what her reaction is. This can be replayed to see which version creates the most effective scene.

Conclusion

What started as an MotE experiment ended up being a really good stimulus lesson for Year 7s. It has since gone on to be used by English staff at our Academy, who are trying to improve writing in their gothic horror scheme (Year 10).

I have since worked with science and humanities on other projects and plan to work with the music department. I have taken these ideas into local feeder schools where they have been met with much enthusiasm. Mantle of the Expert remains for me very much a 'watch this space' curriculum tool. I look forward to further promoting drama to other departments and feeder schools, and to using it to further raise the profile of what drama can do within our Academy.

For anyone interested in learning more about Mantle of the Expert, please visit the excellent www. mantleoftheexpert.com website. Even better, go to one of their training weekends.

The school production

Mark Wheeller as Bill Sykes in Marlwood School's production of *Oliver!* It made such an impression on Mark that he named his first-born son Oliver.

They always say, 'save the best 'til last' and so it is with this book. Please do not see this chapter as an add-on, in the same way so many people see the school production. This may happen at the end of a busy day and the end of term but I maintain that the school production is the key to a thriving drama department! It is probably true that all schools who have outstanding drama departments have outstanding school productions. However, it is frequently a separate event that bears little or no relation to what occurs in the drama curriculum. In some schools, sadly, it becomes a chore.

For me, the school production is the backbone of my work; probably because it is where my interest in drama started. I look back on the productions I did when I was a student and they were the high points in my school life; such productions *can* and often *do* provide high points in young people's lives. This realisation was not some great discovery on my part, but is a belief I have formed having reflected on my own experience, as is the case with much of my work. So, here's my story, and with it my 'theory' – if that's the right word – as to why a quality school production is crucially important to a successful drama department.

I have already referred to productions I did at my own school and college in the opening chapter, but then went on to talk about my curriculum work in my first job at Stantonbury. There was a growing feeling among young drama teachers that the school production was not what a drama teacher was there to do. I remember other students at college saying they weren't going to do the school production – it was too much for them on top of their day job and it had nothing to do with the work they were planning to do in curriculum time. I remember being berated by another student teacher for defending such productions. So, against all advice from those around me I put on a full-scale school production in my first term at Stantonbury. People were fearful that I would not cope with the demands of a full teaching day and then staying on for a couple of hours, not to mention the evenings of planning, but I wouldn't have had it any other way.

Productions were the one thing I knew how to do. I hadn't got a clue about teaching at that point and was literally learning as an apprentice, day by day! In many ways, directing the production was relaxing. It had always been my hobby. I was in control and was still managing to ensure that more of my new songs were performed. My first production at Stantonbury was particularly special as I was granted permission to adapt Mordecai Richler's wonderful book *Jacob Two-Two meets the Hooded Fang.*[1] The book has since been serialised and developed into a successful CITV programme.

Putting on this production allowed me to gain powerful support across the year groups within the student population. Many were in classes I taught and it made an incredible difference to my relationships with them and, as a result of that, with others in their class.

---

1.   My musical version written with *Sunday Times* sports editor Nick Mason (script and lyrics) remains unpublished; it was called *Child Power*.

This school production was actually helping with what has become known in recent years as behaviour management. Those in the production who weren't in my class would greet me as I walked (back then, mostly ran) from class to class. It had a profound effect on my profile on the campus. The production had a cast of about 70 and was seen by about 700 people. I built relationships with parents and other staff who became involved; it helped me become an 'established' teacher within my first term.

No other subject has the opportunity to show off its wares so publicly than drama, so it is an opportunity not to be missed. I was determined to make the most of it and the majority of people admired what I was doing. This school production, far from being an add-on, became my security blanket and made my teaching more effective because students engaged with me.

After *Child Power* I faced a problem: Nick, my then co-writer, lived in London and I was in Milton Keynes. He had a family and a high-pressure job so was never going to be able to write a new script for our next show which I was eager to start as soon as possible. I didn't feel confident enough to write a script myself so, necessity being the mother of invention, I decided to invite a group of students to write a musical together; it needed little planning, would be fun and still allowed me to be responsible for the song-writing.

The group was selected mainly from the *Child Power* cast. I worked with them after school over two terms to create a musical using three songs I had written for a 4R production about World War II. I wanted to have a large cast so the evacuation was an obvious subject matter. This gave us a basic set of ideas and constraints (always a good thing in with story-building) and after talking to parents, we managed to develop an interesting factional story, which we cast and then improvised. When each scene was 'ready' I recorded it onto a cassette tape (showing my age now!) and a couple of us transcribed it by hand. For the first time in my life I took on responsibility for a script, making sure it 'worked'. I found I really enjoyed it – the playwriting seed was sewn. Two terms later we had our own musical, *Blackout*!

The sense of ownership and shared achievement amongst the group was phenomenal. The students who had improvised the scenes with me were genuine collaborators which affected the whole teacher/student relationship. (I have remained in regular contact with many of this group, 30 years on). It emphasised the importance of using first names, as we did at Stantonbury – students were treated as colleagues. I feel strongly that this would have been detrimentally affected by one of the group having to be called Sir or some other self-aggrandising title. [2]

When we came to cast *Blackout,* some of the improvisers were unable to participate so we auditioned the major roles and, of course, the large chorus; over 100 students auditioned for the production.

My best actors were not necessarily the best singers, yet in standard musicals the central characters all sing. In *Blackout,* Mark Eagle – who created the George Eagle part – was not a singer at all! As a direct consequence of that, George Eagle was not given any songs; he had just one line in the title song, which he could talk/sing. We also had a couple of amazing singers who

---

2.   I recently said if there were one thing I could bequeath to the English school system it would be the use of first names between teachers and students. It is so much more natural in my view. It is beginning to happen with politicians and doctors ... why not teachers?

didn't want to act so I wrote a number of songs for them that they sang as narrator figures from the side of stage. This became a feature of my musicals and makes them especially suitable for casting in schools.

I continued to stage musicals – as many as two a year – and masses of youngsters became involved. Then, one day, following one of the productions (*Smike*, the only non-original I did), James Fishwick, the drama teacher I'd team-taught with every week, made a comment to me, questioning what the students were gaining from the productions:

'Well, if you gave them sweets they'd enjoy them … but theatre is about more than just enjoying yourself.'

I was taken aback by the bluntness of his comment. At the time I put it down to jealousy of the very positive relationships I had built up with the cast, but it nagged at me … did he have a point? I began to question what these musicals I directed actually did. This is what I came up with:

>> They established me faster as a well-respected teacher.
>> Those which were collaboratively created offered a positively creative experience where a core of students gained an understanding of theatre that no hour-a-week lesson could give them.
>> *Blackout* explored dilemmas faced by ordinary people in World War II, which was surely of value. The girl who created the part of Rachel said that the story helped her as it mirrored the family break-up she was experiencing at the time.
>> Productions such as *Smike* (the one in the firing line for the 'sweets' criticism) proved an effective way of introducing literary classics in the way that *Oliver!* did for me when I was at school; *Oliver Twist* remains one of the few literary classics I have read from cover to cover.
>> *Fame Game*, the venture after *Blackout!*, used the song-writing skills of the cast to the extent that I did myself out of job of writing them myself, but it was excellent practise.
>> These productions involved many students the school found difficult to manage. This made them feel better about themselves and in many cases improved their aspirations in life, not just at school in drama.

No, I couldn't accept that my productions were simply providing 'enjoyment' and carried little real value for our students. A link I failed to make at that point was that, not only could these productions make an impact on my lessons in terms of attitudes and relationships but it could also be an opportunity to teach specific theatre craft. What I was asking students to do in lessons bore little relationship to what I was spending so much time doing in these school productions, yet here I had a captive audience (the cast) made up of the school's most motivated students in drama.

The other aspect of the productions that I started to question was whether all the effort was worth it for a mere three nights of performances? These productions were a lot of effort and many people were saying I would burn myself out if I wasn't careful. Finding a solution to these two problems means that, in the 25 years that followed, I became much more aware of how to harness the potential of the school production.

I took Roy Nevitt's documentary theatre ideas with me to Epping and put on a new version of *Blackout* [3] (again in my first term), this time interspersed with interviews with four evacuees who spoke of their experiences in the real evacuation. These comments gave an authenticity to the fictional story that wasn't in the in the original production. The success of this was broadcast far and wide; the Times Educational Supplement had this to say about it:

---

3. A further version of *Blackout* is now available from *www.SchoolplayProductions.co.uk* as a download. This version incorporates the oral testimony as part of the (improved) script. It is now one of my most-performed school musicals.

'The evocation of the period was so good that I spent the first act waiting for Vera Lynn's entrance.'   Hugh David, TES.

This gave me the confidence to develop my first documentary play. I chose as my subject the local (to Epping) international blind athlete, Graham Salmon. As with *Blackout,* I selected a core group of students who would work closely with me to research, write and perform this play. We knew we were going to have a lot of work to do and decided from the outset that we shouldn't merely perform it for three nights in our school hall. We decided to tour it to other venues (e.g. Graham's former school), to do fundraising and finally, take it to the Edinburgh Fringe Festival where we would perform six days in one week.

Mark Wheeller (right) with Graham Salmon, the subject of his play: *Graham – World's Fastest Blind Runner*

What I hadn't realised was how much this would raise the profile of a production. People say that putting on productions that are not well-known cannot generate the same level interest of something like *Oliver!* but I totally refute this. *Race to be Seen,*[4] as this production came to be known, attracted massive audiences and considerable local and national television news coverage[5]. This has been true of a number of my other productions, before my work became better-known. Another school who did *Race to be Seen* before it was published gained a two page feature in the *Times Educational Supplement.* We performed it six times on our home territory and sold out each time. We did a further 10 or so productions on the road. This felt a much better reward for the hours of preparation we had put into it. We were also able to attract an audience of more than just parents and friends and this continues to be the case for all my new plays.

Taking a production to festivals

The Edinburgh Fringe Festival was an incredible experience for all of us involved in *Race to be Seen.* Not only did we have the opportunity to perform our play and gain national reviews (we became the Scottish Evening News *Critic's Choice*) but we also had the opportunity to see the best up-and-coming theatre of the day, which would in-turn inspire any work we went on to do. That year (1984) we saw John Godber's premiere productions of both *Up and Under* and *Bouncers,* a very complete education on minimal stagecraft. We felt for the first time we were part of a bigger world and this affected all our aspirations. I have rarely wanted to do a three night run with a play following this experience, and so made it my business to discover other Festivals we could tap into.

I entered *Too Much Punch for Judy*[6] (my final Epping production in 1987) into the National Student Drama Festival (NSDF). Although we were 'highly commended' we were not invited to perform at this prestigious event in Scarborough. Though, like the incy-wincy spider, I tried again and six years later Oaklands Youth Theatre (OYT) performed *Chunnel of Love*[7] at the NSDF. I have tried since, but this remains the only production I have had selected for this festival.[8]

---

4.   *Race to be Seen* was rewritten as a one act play in 2008 entitled *Graham – World's Fastest Blind Runner.* Oaklands Youth Theatre's performance of the play (now on dvd available from dbda) became a finalist in the *All England Theatre Festival* one act play competition.

5.   *Race* was featured on ITV and BBC local news programmes, BBC Nationwide and both the Breakfast TV channels at the time as well as radio and newspapers.

6.   *Too Much Punch for Judy* is now published by dbda.

7.   *Chunnel of Love* a bi-lingual play about an unplanned pregnancy on a French exchange is now published by www.zigzageducation.co.uk and available as a download.

8.   The NSDF have changed their rules and at the time of writing do not allow school-age students to enter plays or attend the festival. A disappointing decision in my view.

In 1989 the Royal National Theatre established the Lloyds Bank Theatre Challenge[9] and on our first attempt OYT were invited to perform *Hard to Swallow*[10] on the Olivier Stage at the National Theatre. In fact, we performed there on the occasion of Lord Olivier's death which is an incredible thing to be able to say. When we entered that competition I was disappointed by the prospect of that as a prize – I remember saying: 'I'd rather they gave us a video camera.' I have never been more wrong. That occasion remains, along with my wedding, one of the highlights of my life. The prestige of the event also led to a number of other things: my literary agency saw the performance and as a result, offered to represent me, and still do; Ginny Spooner, now chief examiner for Edexcel, saw the production and later did much to enthuse teachers about my plays as ideal GCSE drama pieces once they were published. I still meet people who say they were there and it was their introduction to my work. Not only that, but OYT was invited to tour the play in Texas ... all expenses paid!

I love the competitive nature of these festivals (something other drama teachers occasionally vociferously disapprove of). I would hate anyone to think that I only like them because we have achieved success; we have had to deal with our share of failure. I remember an appalling review for *Hard to Swallow* (then titled *Catherine*) at the Edinburgh Fringe Festival:

> 'It is a formulaic Fringe show – biography, social commentary, dance routines and songs surround the death of Catherine. I found the whole business, apart from despair for the central character, exploitative.'
>
> Hayden Murphy, The Scotsman

I have yet to win *The Scotsman* over with my work.

Of all the festivals, the All England Theatre Festival (AETF[11]) has become my favourite. The AETF has many advantages and it is sad that more schools do not get involved. It has the reputation of being somewhat old fashioned but there is so much to be gained from it. It is set at a local level but also offers the opportunity to progress onto a national stage. Our first round is in Totton, about five miles from our base, where around 12 groups normally perform. About 25% of performances are youth plays, and rules stipulate they must last between 20 and 55 minutes. The standard in our region is impressive and the range of styles performed, wide. It is a valuable opportunity to get to know other plays and see other companies at work. Once again it places your own work in a context that is larger than your own school.

Most importantly the AETF offers an instant and very detailed public adjudication from an experienced adjudicator. They comment on the staging of the play and each individual performance. At worst, it is another voice telling the cast the same message you have been trying to deliver in the rehearsal period. At best, it is helpful comments which I would never have thought of. An example of this was with our performance of *Missing Dan Nolan* at one AETF, where the adjudicator directed some comments at the writing of the play. She said that the end needed to be the moment of Dan's disappearance. I hadn't done this originally as it wasn't the last thing to happen in the chronology of the story, but this comment did open my eyes to the fact that the chronology could be experimented with. As a consequence the play was restructured and greatly improved. When we entered it for the Woking Drama Festival – the largest in the UK – we won the award for the best youth production against some outstanding competition.

As testimony to the power of touring school productions, my plays have been adopted by professional companies as the demand is too high for us to fulfil. Here is a comment from a former student about what the experience meant to her:

> 'When I was in Year 10 I had my meeting with the careers advisor. I told her I wanted to work in television as a researcher and was very quickly told that people like me don't do jobs like that and maybe I should consider childcare as a career. Through OYT's participation

---

9.   This was the forerunner to the National Connections scheme that runs today (2010).

10.   *Hard To Swallow* is now published by dbda.

11.   www.aetf.org.uk.

in festivals I had been lucky enough to meet a lot of people who had interesting jobs in the world of media and theatre and I realised they were just normal people who had a passion for something that they turned into their job. This inspired me hugely. I went on to become a television researcher and then a producer – a career that led me to travel a lot and meet some amazing people.'

Carley Wilson, former OYT member

The cast of OYT's One Million to STOP THE TRAFFIK on the evening they became English champions in the AETF 2010

Individuals in the cast also get great advice from these adjudications – and also awards! Best Youth Performer is a much-coveted award and I'm pleased to say some of my youth theatre members over the years have won it. An award, even at a local amateur drama festival does a world of good for a one's self esteem. I have only recently achieved major success at the AETF; at the time of writing (2010), Oasis Youth Theatre's most recent production *One Million to STOP THE TRAFFIK* is representing England in the British Final.[12]

A model for curriculum performance work

The other opportunity the school production (or youth theatre[13] performance) offers is to model a wide range of transferable skills/techniques, which can go on to be used in curriculum theatre performance work. This came about as a result of my perseverance in working on what I call 'impossible scenes'.

I knew it was going to be impossible to present a play about Graham Salmon without showing races. It seemed equally impossible to stage them, particularly the final exciting 400 metres race. However, I was determined to tell Graham's story and to do so we had work around this. The same applied to the crash scene in *Too Much Punch for Judy,* and countless others we would later stage. None of these scenes arrived with instructions. There were no templates that we knew about. Necessity is the mother of invention and so it was with these scenes.

I can remember making Mike Mears (Graham in OYT's award winning production of *Graham World's Fastest Blind Runner)* run on the spot in front of the rest of the cast to test my contention that, if we see someone on stage wearing themselves out it affects our physiology and so we can empathise with the their tiredness. Further than that, I believed (rightly) that this would affect our breathing. It led to an original way of staging the climatic 400 metres World Championship race, where Graham finally wins a gold medal.[14]

I remember bringing melons and choppers into *Too Much Punch* rehearsals, feeling that somehow the destruction of a melon would provide us with a gory image to suggest the pulverisation of someone's head in a decapitation! In the end melons were

12.   *One Million to STOP THE TRAFFIK*: the script and DVD are available from dbda publishers. Image reproduced by kind permission of www.asmagazine.co.uk.

13.   The model of youth theatre at our academy is an interesting one. We are an 11–16 Academy. The youth theatre is a community outreach group. We are able to augment the students from our school with locals who are older (or younger). The older performers are invaluable role models to younger students. They raise the bar in terms of what young people feel they can achieve. We also have school productions, which are specifically for Gifted and Talented students. They may involve a very small, select group and so are ideal for festivals. These all work alongside the more standard school musical production. There is room for everything.

14.   This scene can be seen on the DVD of OYT'S production published by dbda.

abandoned. The trick on my part has been to seem confident that there is a solution … even when I'm scared stiff there isn't! Through genuine co-constructive learning, in many cases, students tell me how to solve the problems. This kind of work produced a core of students in my classes who became expert at developing highly-imaginative solutions to very complicated scenes without realising what they had achieved. As a consequence of this, the standard of devised work improved and more students achieved the highest grades. I remember a fantastic staging of the moors murderers, the Hillsborough disaster and various versions of *Jack and the Beanstalk*, which led to the creation of my own *Kill Jill*). Examiners would describe our candidates as having a 'house style', but it was obviously a house style of which they thoroughly approved.

Once I became aware this style was enhancing achievement, I decided quite consciously to write a musical with a script like one of my stylistically-interesting plays i.e. laden with techniques. *No Place for a Girl*[15] (songs by Brian Price, the music teacher at the time) drew everything together; a musical where none of the main roles had any singing to do (so I could use my best actors and the music teacher could select the best singers for the singing, non-acting parts) and the chorus were busy on stage with imaginative set pieces. (There is no better behaviour-management strategy in rehearsals than keeping the chorus challenged/occupied.)

This musical offers the opportunity for a large cast to be involved in an imaginative presentation and remains, in my view, my undiscovered gem. I wrote it to be my 'hit' musical (describing it in the blurb as a *Zigger Zagger* for boys AND girls) with these specifically school-friendly ingredients and yet it has only been performed by a handful of different schools.

GCSE groups in schools, other than ours, started to present edited versions of my plays for their exams, and soon they were becoming highlighted as being among the most popular plays used in the Edexcel GCSE exam; however I was not using them with my own candidates. When we later 'allowed' our students to use my scripts, creating outstanding performances became much easier/safer. Because my plays are borne out of a devised tradition of school drama, they naturally have a quality that suits students' work for the exam.

I look back on the work my candidates produced over the years and the most exciting was the devised work of my high-ability students in the 80s and 90s – but it was hard, hard work; possibly too hard for GCSE. Also, in those years the C/D/E candidates were not always best-served by being pushed towards the devised option. They are, without doubt, assisted to a better result (grade-wise and artistically) by the support of a good, imaginative script. My reservations about the script work for the most able at GCSE level is that it can become a colouring-by-numbers exercise. However, our best marks (if that is how work is to be finally judged) have been achieved most consistently in the noughties, where script work has been very much to the fore.

In recent years, the productions I have directed with OYT have become templates for future GCSE exam pieces. The link between school and youth theatre productions is obvious for all to see and is like an ongoing snowball effect, constantly improving the best efforts of the previous year. If our school productions comprised exclusively of well-known musicals we would be missing a trick; thankfully, in a multi-teacher department such as ours, we do not have to make that choice. Famous musical productions have much value – I still adore *Oliver!* – but if I were alone in a department and had to choose between one that supports what I do in the curriculum or a classic musical, it would always be the former.

Our productions really do provide the backbone to the standard of theatrical performance in our academy. I don't look back on my early musical ventures as purely offering sweets to the cast, but perhaps I was a long way from exploiting the full potential of the school production. Yes, my colleague James did have a point in his comments about my early productions … although it has taken me a long while to admit it!

---

15.   *No Place for a Girl* is available on download from www.schoolplayproductions.co.uk